LIEGE

LUXEMBOURG

Bouillon

Sedan

Meuse

Verdun

Metz

LORRAINE

ALSACE

Saint-Mihiel

Bar-le-Duc

Toul

Orbey

Rhin

BASSIGNY

Chaumont

Ferrette

BRESSE

FRANCHE-COMTÉ

Rhône

DAUPHINÉ

PROVENCE

BOURGOGNE

GERMANY

SWITZERLAND

ITALY

The Coutumes
of France
in the Library
of Congress

Courtroom scene, folio 2. Twelve men meet with court officials to decide a case. Decisions made by twelve men are mentioned several times in the *Coustumes de Normandie,* as in a section on solving quarrels over fiefs: "Enqueste est recognoissant de verite de la chose quoy contens est par le serment de xij hoͦmes chevalliers ou aultres proudes hoͦmes creables qui ne soient pas souppeconͦeus a lune partie et a lautre." (folio 144)

The Coutumes
of France
in the Library
of Congress

An Annotated Bibliography

by

Jean Caswell and Ivan Sipkov

with the editorial assistance of
Natalie Gawdiak

European Law Division
Law Library

Library of Congress   Washington   1977

Library of Congress Cataloging in Publication Data

United States.   Library of Congress.   European Law
    Division.
    The coutumes of France in the Library of Congress.

    Bibliography: p.
    Includes index.
    1.   Customary law—France—Bibliography.   I.   Caswell,
Jean.   II.   Sipkov, Ivan, 1917–   III.   Title.
Law   016.34′00944   76-608412
ISBN 0-8444-0232-X

For sale by the Superintendent of Documents, U.S. Government Printing Office
Washington, D.C. 20402

Stock No. 030–001–00083–4

Contents

Foreword vii
Preface ix
Note on the Illustrations xi
Introduction 3
General Coutumes of France 7
Coutume Regions (Pays de coutume) 13
  Coutumes of the Central Region 13
    Auvergne 13
    Auxerre 14
    Beauvaisis 15
    Berry 15
    Blois 17
    Bourbonnais 17
    Bourges 18
    Chartres 18
    Clermont-en-Beauvaisis 18
    Etampes 18
    Loir-et-Cher 18
    Lorris 18
    Mantes 19
    Marche 20
    Meaux 20
    Melun 20
    Montargis 20
    Montfort-l'Amaury 20
    Nivernais 20
    Orléans 21
    Paris 22
    Perche 25
    Senlis 25
    Touraine 26
    Tours 26
  Coutumes of the Western Region 29
    Angers 29
    Angoumois 29
    Anjou 29
    Brittany 30
    La Rochelle 33
    Loudun 33
    Maine 33
    Morbihan 34
    Normandy 34

Poitou 37
Roville 39
Coutumes of the Northern Region 41
  Abbeville 41
  Amiens 41
  Arras 42
  Artois 42
  Bailleul 42
  Bouillon 42
  Cambrai 43
  Châlons 43
  Flanders 43
  Gorgue 44
  Guines 44
  Hainaut 44
  Lille 45
  Luxembourg 45
  Mons 46
  Peronne 46
  Picardy 46
  Ponthieu 46
  Reims 47
  Saint-Amand 47
  Saint-Bauzeil 47
  Saint-Omer 47
  Sedan 47
  Tournai 47
  Vermandois 48
Coutumes of the Eastern Region 51
  Alsace 51
  Bar-le-Duc 51
  Bassigny 51
  Bresse 51
  Burgundy 51
  Champagne 54
  Chaumont-en-Bassigny 54
  Ferrette 54
  Franche-Comté 55
  Lorraine 55
  Lorraine and Bar 55
  Metz 55
  val d'Orbey 56

Saint-Mihiel 56
Sens 56
Troyes 57
Vaudémont 57
Verdun 58
Vitry-en-Perthois 58
Coutumes of Written Law Regions (Pays de
    droit écrit) 61
Agen 61
Andorre 61
Béarn 61
Bordeaux 62
Castel-Amouroux 62
Castelsagrat 62
Dauphine 63
Laroque-Timbaut 63

Prayssas 63
Provence 63
Roussillon 63
Saint-Gauzens 64
Saint-Jean-d'Angély 64
Toulouse 64
Appendixes 67
Glossary of Geographic Terms 67
Rulers of France (751–1852) 69
Emperors of the Holy Roman Empire ... 70
Selected Bibliography 71
Indexes 73
Names Cited in the Text 73
Author and Compiler Index 75
Printer, Publisher, and Vendor Index 78

Foreword

The Law Library maintains the world's largest legal collection of American, foreign, and international law materials and employs a staff of experts whose primary task is to provide legal reference and research services to Congress. In addition to this important function, the Law Library legal staff also periodically prepares and publishes reference works which are meant to describe the Law Library holdings and to assist scholars in their studies of various aspects of law.

The present bibliography is such a work and has been undertaken to make available, in a systematic order, a listing of one of the Law Library's special collections. The coutumes, or French local customary laws, played an important role in the development of the modern French legal system. A knowledge of these laws is also important in the study of the legal development of the various French colonies in America, especially in the state of Louisiana, and in other parts of the world.

Carleton W. Kenyon
Law Librarian

Preface

Among the several special collections—Canon Law, Consilia, Roman Law, Incunabula, Manuscripts, Feudal Law, etc.—in the custody of the European Law Division of the Law Library, there is a collection of the coutumes, or customary laws, of Andorra, Belgium, France, Italy, Luxembourg, the Netherlands, Switzerland, and other countries.

Originally these coutumes were incorporated in the holdings of the various countries in the European Law Division collections. Over the years, however, the number of the coutumes of France increased to such an extent that the formation of a separate collection was deemed necessary to provide a more convenient organization for their study by scholars and students of the droit coutumier. At first the collection was meant to comprise only French coutumes, but the coutumes of other European countries were added subsequently because of their close relationship to the French customary codes.

The following bibliography attempts to include the entire French coutumes collection within the jurisdiction of the European Law Division of the Law Library of Congress. An effort will be made in the future to cover also coutumes maintained in the other departments of the Library of Congress as well as the coutumes of countries other than France.

The materials have been arranged in three major groups: General Coutumes of France, Coutume Regions (pays de coutume), and Coutumes of Written Law Regions (pays de droit écrit). The pays de coutume are further subdivided into central, western, northern, and eastern, in accordance with the classification scheme of Ernest D. Glasson, on whose work this bibliography is primarily based.

For convenient reference, all of the coutumes listed are numbered consecutively, and cross-references are used to avoid repeating an item that falls within several categories. When there is more than one coutume for a city or region, works are listed chronologically by date of publication under their "short titles." The names of the authors, compilers, editors, publishers, printers, and places of publication are included in the entries. Due to their importance, five manuscripts and two incunabula which contain French coutumes but are not located in the Law Library main coutumes collection have also been included in this bibliography. In addition, customary law holdings available on microfilm in the Library of Congress are indicated by a list of dates at the end of each section.

A glossary of geographical terms as they appear in the titles of the various coutumes is given to assist those unfamiliar with these terms. An author index and a printer, publisher, and vendor index have been appended for reference and to furnish the scholar and reader with the modern English spelling of original French and Latin names. In some instances, however, certain names may be listed in their original forms because no established modern English names could be determined. In addition, a separate index of personal names appearing in the text of the bibliography is given for further convenience. Finally, tables of the rulers of France and the emperors of the Holy Roman Empire as well as a map showing customary law jurisdictions in old France and a short bibliography of reference materials are attached.

As the present bibliography is the first of its kind to be published in this country, it is certain to have some shortcomings. We hope, however, that this work will be a useful basis for further studies.

Jean Caswell
Ivan Sipkov

Note on the Illustrations

The map on the endsheets shows the major regions and cities mentioned in the text.

The seven color illustrations are from the *Coustumes de Normandie* (no. 263 in the bibliography), an unusual and appealing manuscript copy of the *Grand Coutumier de Normandie.* Although a number of manuscript coutumiers still exist, most of them, if decorated at all, have only colored rubrics announcing each chapter. The Library of Congress manuscript is embellished with elegant flourish initials, line endings, painted initials, and seven handsomely bordered miniatures.

The manuscript is regular in its physical composition. Most of the gatherings are in quires of eight. One skillful scribe seems to have written the entire manuscript, and the miniatures all appear to be the work of one hand.

The artist who painted the miniatures followed the contemporary conventions and techniques, but with a distinct individuality. He used bright, clear colors in a flat, decorative way. Unlike many other artists of that time, he showed no interest in atmospheric perspective. His style is loosely related to that associated with a group of manuscripts gathered around the name of Maître François, but the *Coustumes* master cannot be assumed to be a member of that circle. The works most closely comparable to the *Coustumes* miniatures appear in the *Queen Medusa Enthroned* miniature in the Cleveland Museum, and in the *Roman de la Rose* (Oxford, Bodleian Library, Ms. Douce 364).

The temptation is great to localize the production of this book in a Norman workshop simply because the *Coustumes* are for Normandy. More solid justification for a Norman origin can be found, however, in the page layout and borders, which are as useful in identifying an atelier as the miniatures themselves. Codicological similarities between the Library of Congress *Coustumes de Normandie* and its *Horae* Ms. 174, with Evreux Use and Evreux saints; between the *Coustumes* and the Pierpont Morgan *Coutumier de Normandie* Ms. M 457, with its Rouen saints; and between the *Coustumes* and Waddesden Manor Ms. 12, a Book of Hours for Rouen Use, suggest a related provenance for this manuscript—either an atelier in Normandy, or one that produced books for use in Normandy.

A date on folio 239r of the *Coustumes* reads "le xix^e jour du mois de mars lan mil cccc et xiiii" (19 March 1414). This date does not accord with the style of the miniatures and must be a scribe's error in copying the text date of 19 March 1314, the historical date of the *Charte aux Normands,* which ends on that same folio. The date of the Library of Congress manuscript can be approximated by comparing the *Coustumes* codicologically and stylistically with other manuscripts, such as those used in the above comparisons. In spite of the archaic script, a date of production in the third quarter of the fifteenth century is suggested.

The Coutumes
of France
in the Library
of Congress

Introduction

The coutumes, a primary source of modern French law, were originally local customary laws. They were the chief laws of the pays de coutume, i.e., the central and northern part of France, where the parlements, acting as sovereign judicial bodies independent from each other, rendered their decisions based on the legal principles derived from these local customs and privileges.[1] On the other hand, the pays de droit écrit, corresponding to the Midi, were those areas in which Roman law dominated. Ernest Glasson emphasized, however, that even in the pays de droit écrit, the importance of Roman law should not be exaggerated, because coutumes did develop in those southern regions, and they often contradicted Roman law.[2]

The term *coutume* refers to both the customary laws and usages of a region and to any collection of these laws. Although not originally collected systematically, coutumes were sometimes recorded in the charters of franchises or of communes granted by the king or by lords as early as the eleventh century.[3] Because the coutumes grew out of daily life and custom, the ensuing droit coutumier was truly indigenous and met the needs of contemporary life. However, as a legal system, droit coutumier often lacked precision and varied greatly from region to region. Another disadvantage of droit coutumier before the codification of the coutumes was the complicated procedure necessary to establish a coutume.[4] To be accepted as coutumes, usages coutumiers had to show certain characteristics. They had to be *généraux* (in the territory in which applied), *multipliés* (applied often enough to constitute established habit), *anciens* (required age varied, but was often forty years), and *constants* (uninterrupted).[5] To test a coutume for acceptance or to establish its true meaning, an inquest by a turbe was necessary. A turbe was made up of twelve to thirty witnesses (*sages hommes*). The members of the turbe elected a chairman to speak for them, and any decision had to be unanimous. Two obvious disadvantages of the inquest by turbe were the expense of calling so many witnesses and the strong possibility that a session would fail to reach an agreement.[6]

Because coutumes were numerous and varied, and because the establishment of their validity through turbes was so costly in time and money, some legal practitioners (lawyers, baillis, and other government officials) collected the coutumes which were in force in their region.[7] These collections, called coutumiers or anciennes coutumes, were purely private works, but some of them attained the force of law through use.[8] Examples are the *Grand Coutumier de Normandie* of ca. 1254–58 (nos. 263, 264), and Philippe de Beaumanoir's *Coutumes du comté de Clermont en Beauvaisis,* ca. 1283 (nos. 65–67). Although it was unofficial, the *Grand Coutumier de Normandie* continued to be applied until, in answer to royal letters of 1577, the official redaction of the *Coutume de Normandie* took place in 1583.[9]

Charles VII responded to the need for a systematic collection of French coutumes in the decisive article 125 of an ordinance delivered at Montil-lès-Tours in April 1453 (O.S.).[10] He ordered that the "coustumes, usages et stiles" of all the countries in his realm be drawn up by the people of each region, written in books which would be brought before the king, examined by members of his grand conseil or of his parlement, and decreed and confirmed by the king.[11] This codification program was carried on in various forms by later monarchs for three and a half centuries.[12] At first, progress was slow because of the complex procedure outlined by Charles VII, but this procedure was simplified by several of his successors. For example, Charles VIII, in letters patent of March 15, 1498 (N.S.), declared that the articles already agreed upon by those charged with the drafting of the coutume did not have to be verified by his parlement.[13]

The influence of Charles VII's ordinance extended beyond his realm and his time. On March

3

11, 1457, in Bruges, Philip the Good, duke of Burgundy, issued letters patent ordering the redaction of the coutumes of his land. The coutumes of both the duchy and the county of Burgundy were confirmed in 1459.[14]

After codification, the exact text of any coutume could be verified by referring to the copy which was deposited with the record office of the parlement or the court of the sovereign. According to Glasson, more than 400 coutumes were officially recognized; approximately sixty of these were coutumes générales; the rest were coutumes locales. The application of each of the general and local coutumes was limited to a definite area.[15] As a rule, each local coutume was included within the territory of a general coutume, but the local coutume could prevail over the general. A coutume could not contradict a royal ordinance, and it could be derogated by such an ordinance.[16] Roman law was applied when the local and general coutumes were silent.[17]

The coutumes are of interest to legal scholars concerned with the formation of law. The officially compiled and published coutumes supplied the foundations for French legal doctrines and paved the way for the codification undertaken by Napoleon. Many basic concepts of the Code Napoléon were, in fact, taken from the codified coutumes. The coutumes of Normandy are especially interesting because of the reciprocal influence that existed between the customary law of Normandy and the law of England. The Norman and Parisian coutumes and the later Code Napoléon are of particular importance to American lawyers, for these were introduced into the French colonies and consequently into the law of the modern state of Louisiana. The law relating to community property, for example, is based to a great extent on the rules of the *Coutume de Paris*.[18] Furthermore, approximately 1,800 of the 2,281 articles in the Code Napoléon are contained, in full or in part, in the State of Louisiana Civil Code of 1870. Most of these appear without substantive change.[19] In addition, because Louisiana is a civil law state whose code is based on the Code Napoléon, it has relied heavily upon the writings of French legal scholars for the doctrinal discussions which are so necessary to a logical interpretation and consistent development of a code of general law.[20]

The coutumes are also valuable to historians as a rich source of information about medieval customs. They reveal a lively image of France in the Middle Ages.[21]

Notes

1. Adhémar Esmein, *Cours élémentaire d'histoire du droit français,* 11th ed. (Paris: L. Larose et L. Tenin, 1912), p. 42 ff.

2. Ernest D. Glasson, *Histoire du droit et des institutions de la France,* 8 vols. (Paris: F. Pichon, 1891), 4: 14–17.

3. Jean Brissaud, *A General Survey of Events, Sources, Persons and Movements in Continental Legal History,* transl. Rapelje Howell (1912; reprint ed., New York: Augustus M. Kelley, 1968), vol. 3, pt. 1, pp. 221–23.

4. Glasson, 4: 20–22.

5. Maurice Lefebvre, *La Coutume comme source formelle de droit* (Lille: Camille Robbe, 1906), pp. 67–70.

6. Glasson, 4: 20–22.

7. Auguste Lebrun, *La Coutume, ses sources—son autorité en droit privé* (Paris: R. Pichon et R. Durand-Auzias, 1932), p. 71.

8. Glasson, 8: 11. When laws were collected and codified in response to the orders of the ruler, they were usually entitled "coutume" or "coutumes" of the specific region to which they applied. Because, however, many of the books listed in this bibliography are from a very early date, before these terms were used consistently, their titles do not always match the descriptions exactly.

9. Brissaud, pp. 225–26.

10. Glasson spells the name "Montils les Tours," 8: 12. Henry Klimrath, *Etudes sur les coutumes* (Paris: Levrault, 1837), gives dates in Old Style. Glasson usually, though not consistently, gives dates in New Style. All publication dates in the bibliographical listings are, naturally, Old Style and may differ by one year from Glasson's dates quoted in the descriptive introductions to each section.

11. Free translation of a part of article 125 (Klimrath, p. 4): ". . . ordonnons et décernons, déclarons et statuons: que les coustumes, usages et stiles de tous les pays de nostre royaume soyent redigez et mis en escrit, accordez par les coustumiers, praticiens et gens de chascun estat desdiz pays de nostre royaume, lesquelz coustumes, usages et stiles ainsi accordez seront mis et escritz en livres, lesquelz seront apportez pardevers nous, pour les faire veoir et visiter par les gens de nostre grand conseil, ou de nostre parlement, et par nous les décréter et confermer. . . ."

12. Ernest Anderson, *The Renaissance of Legal Science after the Middle Ages* (Copenhagen: Juristforbundets Forlag, 1974), p. 133. Most of the books in this bibliography are examples of coutumes drawn up, published, codified, and reformed according to the orders of Charles VII and later French kings. In many volumes the procès-verbaux are bound with the coutume, and commentaries by legal scholars are often included.

13. Lebrun, p. 72.

14. Klimrath, p. 5.

15. Glasson, 8: 22.

16. Ibid., p. 25.

17. Brissaud, p. 218.

18. Glasson, 8: 12.

19. Ibid., p. 22.

20. Marcel Planiol, *Treatise on the Civil Law* (1959), vol. 1, pt. 1, "Foreword," p. 3.

21. Klimrath, p. 1.

Homage to the king of France, folio 27. One of the twelve witnesses to this ritual homage wears a love knot (usually linking the first initials of a husband and wife) on his thigh. The rarity of illuminated coutumiers and the inclusion of the love knot suggest that the Library of Congress *Coustumes* was a commissioned work rather than a routine workshop product.

General Coutumes of France

Of the fifteen editions of the general coutumiers of France listed by Claude Berroyer, the seventeenth-century French authority in this field, the Law Library holds ten, nos. 1, 2, 3, 4, 8, 9, 14, 21, 24, 29; missing are the editions of 1519, 1526, 1546, 1550, and 1567.[1] This collection also includes many other editions—some with notes and commentary—that were not mentioned by Berroyer.

One of the most important coutumes in this section of the bibliography is the *Grand Coutumier de France* (no. 12). Sometimes known as the *Coutumier de Charles VI*, the official name was *Le Grant Coutumier de France, et instruction de practique et manière de procéder et practiquer ès souveraines cours de Parlement, prévosté et viconté de Paris et autres jurisdictions du royaulme de France.* This compilation was a practical book, at once a civil code, a code of procedure, and a collection of formulae. *The Grand Coutumier de France* comprised four books. Book One was a later summary of the other books and does not appear in the manuscript copies. Book Two contains the first seeds of the coutume of Paris. Book Three is a book of procedure, and Book Four addresses the question of the dispute between ecclesiastical and secular jurisdictions. There are many versions of this coutume; the seven manuscripts described by Edouard Laboulaye and Rodolphe Dareste, for example, include six different texts. Although Laboulaye and Dareste did not know the author or date of the coutume, they were able to ascertain one important fact; namely, there was no reason to call this work the *Coutumier de Charles VI*.[2] The author's identity was discovered by the nineteenth-century historian Léopold Delisle to be Jacques d'Ableiges, who in 1371 was the secretary of Jean, duke of Berry (1340–1416); d'Ableiges subsequently became examiner at the Châtelet, then bailli of Chartres, Saint-Denis, and Evreux. Thus the *Grand Coutumier* was the work of a practicing lawyer who also knew Roman law and coutumes. The *Grand Coutumier de France* remained in force with some modification until the middle of the sixteenth century.[3]

In addition to the *Grand Coutumier de France*, this section of the bibliography includes a number of treatises on customary law in general, as well as some editions of *La Somme rurale de Boutillier*. Henry Beaune considered the *Somme rurale* to be far superior to the *Grand Coutumier de France*. Sometime after 1383, Jean Boutillier, a citizen of Tournai, wrote this compilation of laws for the rural man, the poor, and the commoner. A summary of all the customary law of the fourteenth century, his book is a rich resource for the jurisconsult and historian.[4]

1517

1 Les grādes coustumes generalles et particulieres du rayaulme de France . . . Cestàscauoir les coustumes de la preuoste et viconte de Paris . . . les coustumes de Meaulx, Melun, Victry, Chaumont, Orleans . . . Paris, Ils se vendent sur le pont nostre Dame a lenseigne sainct Jehan leuangeliste, 1517. 430 l.

1522

2 Les grandes coustumes generalles et particulieres du royausme de France . . . Paris, Frãncovs Regnavlt, 1522. 436 l.

1527

3 Les coustumes et statuz . . . du Royaume de Frãce . . . Paris, Iehan Petit, 1527. 578 l.

1536

4 Les coustumes et statutz . . . du Royaulme de Frãce . . . Paris, Galliot du Pré, 1536. 598 l.

1539

5 La grant somme rural du sont contenues deux parties . . . compilee par maistre Jehan Boutillier . . . plusieurs coustumes . . . Paris, Denis Ianot, 1539. 2 pts.

1542

6 Jan Bottelgier heeft dit boeck gemaect. Ende is gheheeten Summe ruyrael . . . Antwerpen, Symon Cock, 1542. 309 p.

1548 (i.e. 1547)

7 Les coustumes et statutz particuliers de la plus-part des bailliages, seneschaucees et preuostez royaulx du royaulme de Frāce . . . Paris, Vend[u] par J. de Roigny, 1548 [i.e. 1547] 588 l.

1552

8 Les coustumes & statutz particuliers de la plvs-part des bailliages . . . de France . . . Paris, Arnoul l'Angelier, 1552. 2 pts.
   See also Burgundy, no. 412 (1565).

1581

9 Des covstvmes generalles et particvlieres dv rayavme de France & des Gaulles . . . Cor-rigees & annotees . . . par Charles dv Movlin & autres iurisconsultes. Paris, I. du Puys, 1581– 2 v.

1585

10 Paraphrase dv droict de retraict lignager, re-cuelle des coustumes de France . . . [par Francois Grimavdet]. Avec vne pref. . . . a Christophle de Thov. Paris, H. de Marnef & la veufue G. Cauellat, 1585. 376 p.

1596

11 La conference des covstvmes tant generales, qve locales et particvlieres dv Rayaume de France . . . annotations par Pierre Gvenoys. Paris, G. Chavdiere, 1596. 2 v. in 1.

1598

12 Le grand covstvmier de France [par Jacques d'Ableiges] . . . diuerses obseruations, par L. Charondas Le Caron . . . Paris, Iean Hovzé, 1598. 562 p.

1603

13 Somme rvral ov le grand covstvmier . . . composé par Iean Bovteiller (. . . par Lovys Charondas le Caron) . . . Paris, Barthelemy Macé, 1603. 904 (i.e. 940) p.

1604

14 Les covstvmes generales et particvlieres de France et des Gavlles, corrigees . . . par Charles du Moulin . . . Auec des Tables . . .

Par Gabriel Michel. Paris, Gvillavme de la Nove, 1604. 2 v.

1607

15 Institvtion av droict des Francois. Par Gvy Coq-ville. Paris, A. L'Angelier, 1607. 364 p.
   Printer's mark on title page.

1607

16 Institvtes covstvmieres. Ov Manvel de plvsievrs et diverses reigles, sentences, & prouerbes . . . du droict coustumier & plus ordinaire de la France. [Par Antoine Loisel] Paris, A. L'Angelier, 1607. 79 p.

1609

17 Institvtion av droict des Francois. Par Gvy Coq-ville. Paris, A. L'Angelier, 1609. 364 p.

1609

18 Institvtes Covstvmieres ov Manvel . . . [par Antoine Loisel]. Paris, Abel L'Angelier, 1609. 79 p.

1609

19 Indice des droicts roiavx et seignevriavx . . . par François Ragveav . . . 3 ed. Paris, Pierre Chevalier, 1609. 595 p.

1611

20 Qvestions et responses svr les covstvmes de France par Gvy Coqville. Paris, Abel L'angelier, 1611. 632 p.

1615

21 Les covstvmes generales et particvlieres de France et des Gavlles. Corrigees et an-notees . . . par Charles du Moulin . . . & autres iurisconsultes. Augmentees & reueuës par Gabriel Michel Angevin . . . Paris, la veufue Marc Ory, 1615. 2 v.
   Publisher's device on title page.

1615

22 Les covstvmes generales et particvlieres de France et des Gavlles. Corrigees et annotees . . . par Charles du Moulin . . . & autres iurisconsultes. Augmentees & reueuës par Gabriel Michel Angevin. Paris, Iean Hovzé, 1615. 2 v.

1621

23 La somme rvral, ov le grand covstvmier . . . par Iean Bovteiller . . . Reueu . . . par

Lovys Charondas le Caron. Lyon, Simon Rigavd, 1621. 1552 p.

1635

24 Les covstvmes generales et particvlières de France et des Gavles, corrigees et annotees . . . par Charles du Moulin. Augmentees & reueuës par Gabriel Michel Angeuin . . . Paris, C. Sonnius, 1635. 2 v.

1644

25 Qvestions et responses svr les articles des covstvmes de France . . . par Gvy Coqville . . . Paris, Edme Pepingvé, 1644. 906 p.

1646

26 Institvtes covstvmieres, ov manvel de plvsievrs et diverses regles . . . du droict coustumier & plus ordinaire de la France. Par Anthoine Loisel. Paris, Henry le Gras, 1646. 164 (i.e. 166) p.
See also Nivernais, no. 121 (1646), and Paris, no. 150 (1652).

1656

27 Institvtes covstvmieres, ov manvel de plvsievrs et diverses regles, . . . du droict coustumier & plus ordinaire de la France. Par Anthoine Loisel, avec les notes et observations de Pavl Challine . . . Paris, Henry le Gras, 1656. 380 p.

1664

28 Les covstvmes generales et particlvlieres de France et des Gavles. Corrigees et annotees . . . par Charles dv Movlin. Augmentées & reueües, par Gabriel Michel Angevin. Paris, I. d'Allin, 1664. 2 v.

1688

29 La jurisprudence . . . les coutumes de France . . . par Claude de Ferriere. Second edition, reveüe, augm. & cor. avec des sommaires. Paris, Jean Cochart, 1688. 2 v.

1699

30 Bibliotheque des coutumes, contenant la preface d'un nouveau coutumier general . . . Le texte des nouvelles coutumes de Bourbonnois corrigé sur l'original, avec les apostils de Charles Du Molin . . . Par Claude Berroyer, & Eusebe de Lauriere . . . Paris, N. Gosselin, 1699. 286 p.
Includes a list of editions of this coutume.

1710

31 Institutes coutumieres de Monsieur Loisel . . . avec des notes nouvelles par Eusebe de Lauriere. Paris, Nicolas Gosselin, 1710. 2 v.

1715

32 Les notes de maistre Charles du Moulin sur les coutumes de France . . . Paris, Denis Mouchet, 1715. 430 p.

1724

33 Nouveau coutumier general, ou Corps des coutumes generales et particulieres de France, et des provinces connues sous le nom des Gaules . . . Avec les notes de Toussaint Chauvelin, Julien Brodeau, & Jean-Marie Ricard . . . Jointes aux annotations de Charles du Molin, François Ragueau, & Gabriel-Michel de la Rochemaillet. Mis en ordre . . . et enrichi de nouvelles notes . . . Par Charles A. Bourdot de Richebourg . . . Paris, T. Le Gras, 1724. 4 v.
See also Paris, no. 169 (1747).

1765

34 Méthode générale pour l'intelligence des coûtumes de France, composée par Maître Paul Challine . . . Douay, Derbaix, 1765. 316 p.
See also Paris, no. 174 (1770), and Angoumois, no. 197 (1780–83).

1846

35 Institutes coutumières d'Antoine Loysel . . . du droit coutumier et plus ordinaire de la France, avec les notes d'Eusèbe de Lauriere. Nouv. éd., rev., cor. et augm., par Dupin . . . et Edouard Laboulaye. Paris, Durand, 1846. 2 v.
"Liste des auteurs et jurisconsultes cités dans les Institutes coutumières": v. 1, p. 91–121.

1868

36 Le grand coutumier de France . . . [par Jacques d'Ableiges] . . . nouv. éd., par Ed. Laboulaye et R. Dareste . . . Paris, Auguste Durand et Pedone-Lauriel, 1868. 848 p.
Includes list and description of manuscripts of Gothic editions.

1880

37 Introduction à l'étude historique du droit coutumier français jusqu'à la rédaction officielle des coutumes, par Henri Beaune . . . Lyon, Briday, 1880. 566 p.

Excellent study of customary law and its roots from the time of the Celts through the sixteenth century.

1882

38 Droit coutumier français; la condition des personnes, par Henri Beaune . . . Lyon, Briday, 1882. 602 p.

1886

39 Droit coutumier français. La condition des biens, par Henri Beaune . . . Paris, Delhomme & Briguet, 1886. 616 p.

1889

40 Droit coutumier français, par Henri Beaune . . . Les contrats. Nouv. éd., rev. et cor. . . . Lyon, Paris, Delhomme et Briguet, 1889. 636 p.

1925

41 La réserve coutumière dans l'ancien droit français, par Jean de Laplanche. Paris, Société anonyme du Recueil Sirey, 1925. 695 p.

1962

42 La Rédaction des coutumes dans le passé et dans le présent. Colloque organisé les 16 et 17 mai 1960 par le Centre d'histoire et d'ethnologie juridiques, sous la direction de John Gilissen. Bruxelles, Université libre de Bruxelles, Institut de sociologie, 1962. 336 p.

History of the compilation of customary law throughout the world.

1966

43 Egalité entre héritiers et exclusion des enfants dotés, essai de géographie coutumière [par Jean Yver] Paris, Sirey, 1966. 310 p.

1969

44 Le grand coutumier de France [par Jacques d'Ableiges] Nouv. éd. par Edouard Laboulaye et Rudolphe Dareste. Réimpr. de l'édition. Paris, 1868. Aalen, Scientia-Verlag, 1969. 848 p.

1972

45 Das Eherecht in den Coutumiers des 13. Jahrhunderts; [Reinald Gräfe] . . . Göttingen, Musterschmidt-Verlag, 1972. 179 p.

Notes

1. Claude Berroyer, *Bibliothèque des coutumes* (Paris: Nicolas Gosselin, 1699), p. 51.
2. See no. 36 of this bibliography, pp. vii–xxii.
3. Ernest D. Glasson, *Histoire du droit et des institutions de la France,* 8 vols. (Paris: F. Pichon, 1891), 4: 155–59.
4. See no. 37 of this bibliography, pp. 441–44.

Execution by hanging, folio 44. This miniature is an example of the adaptation of a religious composition to a secular illustration. It very closely parallels the traditional arrangement of the Descent from the Cross.

Coutume Regions (Pays de coutume)

Coutumes of the Central Region

The coutume jurisdictions in the center of France were divided between north and south, with Paris as the dividing point. The most important coutume in this central region—for the area it governed and the influence it wielded on the formation of other coutumes throughout France—was that of the prévôté and viconté of Paris.[1]

Auvergne

This coutume governed the entire Auvergne region except for those parts which came under the coutume of Bourbonnais or were ruled by droit écrit. In addition, it covered the county of Montpensier and the Haute Marche of Auvergne. There were also many local coutumes in the region.[2]

The compilation of the coutume of Auvergne took place over a long period. Charles VIII ordered the bailli Montferrand to draft the coutume, but these orders were not carried out. Later, similar orders by Louis XII, dispatched to the duchess of Bourbonnais and of Auvergne, led only to conflict between the procurers of the king and of the duchess. Letters with new orders were sent on December 19, 1508, naming the royal commissioners charged with the compilation and publication of the coutume. These orders were renewed in 1510, and on March 1 of that year the coutume of Auvergne was officially recognized by the parlement. The coutume was the work of Chancellor Antoine Duprat,[3] first president, and Picot, counselor to the parlement.[4]

1511(?)
46 Les coustumes de hault & bas pays Dauuergne. Paris, J. Petit [1511?] 64 l.

1548
47 Arvernorvm consvetvdines Ioannis Bessiani . . . Lvgdvni, Apud A. Vincentium, 1548. 248, 47 l.
    Text in French, commentary in Latin.

1548
48 Commentarii in consuetudines Aruerniae, editi per D. Aymonem Publitium . . . Parisiis, Apud Arnoldum Angelier, 1548. 173 l.

1548
49 Commentarii in consuetudines Aruerniae, editi per D. Aymonem Publitium . . . Parisiis, Apud Poncetum Le Preux, 1548. 173 l.
    Text in French, commentary in Latin.
    Device of Poncet Le Preux on title page and at end.

1596
50 Paraphrase de Iean de Basmaison Povgnet sur les coustumes du bas & hault pays d'Auvergne. Avec les annotations de Charles dv Moulin . . . Clermont, I. Dvrand, 1596. 407 p.

1627
51 Les covstvmes locales dv bas et havlt pays d'Auuergne. Clairmont, Bertrand Dvrand, 1627. 135 p.

1628
52 Paraphrases svr les covstvmes dv bas et havlt pays d'Avvergne, par Iean de Basmaison Pougnet. Avec les annotations de Charles dv Molin. 3. ed. Clairmont, Bertrand Dvrand, 1628. 279 p.

1661
53 Joannis Bessiani Annotationes in consuetudine Arvernorum . . . Trajecti ad Rhenum, Typis

13

G. Boschman, bi., 1661. 741 p.
Text in French, commentary in Latin.

1667

54 Covstvmes dv havt et bas pays d'Avvergne, avec la Paraphrase de Iean de Basmaison Pougnet & les notes de Charles Du Molin. 4. ed., rev. & beaucoup augm. par Gvillavme Consvl. Clermont, I. Barbier, 1667. 2 v. in 1.
Corrections on this edition by Consvl Gvillavme.

1695

55 Les Coutumes du Haut et Bas pais d'Auvergne, conferées avec le droit civil, & avec les Coutumes de Paris, de Bourbonnois, de la Marche, de Berri, & de Nivernois. Avec les notes de Charles Du Moulin . . . Par Claude Ignace Prohet. Paris, Jean Guignard, 1695. 340, 103, 31 p.
Brief history of Auvergne included.

1770

56 Coutumes du haut et bas pays d'Auvergne, avec les notes de Charles du Moulin, les observations de Claude-Ignace Prohet, & des explications & interprétations suivant les nouveaux édits . . . par Me. ***, avocat en parlement. Nouv. éd., rev., corr., et augm. des notes de Toussaint Chauvelin, Julien Brodeau, Jean-Marie Ricard & autres-célébres jurisconsultes . . . Clermont-Ferrand, P. Viallanes, 1770. 635 p.

1784–86

57 Coutumes générales et locales de la province d'Auvergne, avec les notes de Charles du Moulin, Toussaint Chauvelin, Julien Brodeau & Jean-Marie Ricard . . . Par Chabrol . . . Riom, Martin Dégouette, 1784–86. 4 v.
Vol. 1 contains a list of different editions of the coutume of Auvergne and related works. Vol. 4 includes a history of Auvergne.

1786 (1974 reprint)

58 Dictionnaire historique des fiefs, châtellenies et paroisses de la Haute et de la Basse Auvergne. Par Chabrol. Tome 4. Riom, Dégouette; Reprint Paris, Librairie Guénégaud, 1974. 1005 p.
Reprint of the 1786 edition published by Dégouette, Riom.

1910

59 La succession ab intestat dans l'ancienne coutume d'Auvergne. Par Jules Lacarrière. Paris, Jouve, 1910. 284 p.

Microfilm: 1538, 1549, 1608, 1627, 1628, 1640, 1745.

Auxerre

The coutume of the bailliage and county of Auxerre applied as well to the bailliage of Sens, to the county of Joigny, to Vézelay, Donzy, Cosne, Saint-Amand, Saint-Saveur, and to several other cities of Donzois and Puisaye. Although Glasson said that it was not certain that the first compilation of the coutume of Auxerre was ever published (because the act ordering that publication has been lost),[5] Edme Billon, lawyer to the parlement, wrote of letters patent of 1506 by Louis XII. The coutume ordered by these letters was compiled and enacted by the Trois Etats, in the presence of Blanchet Dany, lieutenant general of the bailliage, on September 8, 1507. This coutume was in force until 1558, when the people of Auxerre asked that it be reviewed.[6]

Glasson wrote of letters of August 19, 1556, ordering the publication of the coutumes of Poitou and Auxerre, which had already been compiled, but for which the procès-verbaux had been lost. In 1558, Henry II ordered a new compilation of these coutumes,[7] and named as commissioners Christophe de Thou, first president, and Barthélemy Faye and Jacques Violle, counselors of the court of the parlement.[8] Charles IX renewed these orders on January 5 and March 29, 1560, and the new coutume of Auxerre was published in 1561.[9]

1598

60 Covstvmes dv comté et bailliage d'Avcerre . . . Aucerre, Pierre Vatard, 1598. 143 l.

1672

61 Coustumes du comté et bailliage d'Auxerre . . . Auxerre, François Garnier, 1672. 304 p.

1693

62 Coûtume du Comté et Baillage d'Auxerre, avec les nottes . . . par Edme Billon . . . Paris, Jean Guignard, 1693. 568 p.
Preceded by a history of Auxerre.

1743

63 Coutume du comté & bailliage d'Auxerre . . . Nouvelle edition. Auxerre, François Fournier, 1743. 308 p.

   See also Lorris, no. 105 (1758) and no. 106 (1771).

Beauvaisis

Of all the French coutumiers of the thirteenth century, the most remarkable was that of Beauvaisis, composed by the bailli Philippe de Remi, sire de Beaumanoir. Most coutumiers of the time, even that of Normandy, were less complete, and almost all, both before and after Beaumanoir's work, were books of procedure. Beaumanoir, however, succeeded in composing a work which was exclusively customary law.

He proposed, above all, to make known the coutumes of the county of Clermont-en-Beauvaisis, of which he was bailli under Count Robert of France (1256–1317). Beaumanoir's was the most juridical mind of his time, and to the knowledge of law he added its practice. He knew how to temper the rigor of the law with equity, and no part of the law nor institution of his time escaped his investigation. His work was completely original.[10]

Although Philippe de Beaumanoir was a poet, his greatest work was *Coutumes du comté de Clermont en Beauvaisis.* This document was begun around 1280 and finished in 1283, with some additions and corrections made at later dates. The date of 1283, given in the explicit, is therefore only an approximate date.[11]

The coutume of 1496 was an intermediary between the work of Beaumanoir and the coutume of Clermont-en-Beauvaisis[12] which, with the coutumes of Senlis and Valois, was published in 1539 by commissioners André Guillard and Nicole Thibault.[13]

1615

64 Covstvmes de divers bailliages observees en Beavvaisis: Ascavoir de Senlis, Amiens, Clermont & Mondidier, conferées l'une à l'autre & à celle de Paris. Avec notes. Par Pierre Louvet. Beavvais, G. Valet, 1615. 190 p.

   See also Senlis, no. 184 (1631).

1690

65 Coustumes de Beauvoisis, par messire Philippes de Beaumanoir . . . Assises et bons usages du rayaume de Jerusalem, par messire Jean d'Ibelin . . . Et autres anciennes coutumes . . . Par Gaspard Thaumas de la Thaumassiere . . . Bourges, F. Toubeau; et se vend a Paris, en la boutique de L. Billaine, J. Morel, 1690. 2 v. in 1.

   See also Senlis, no. 186 (1703).

1842

66 Les coutumes du Beauvoisis, par Philippe de Beaumanoir . . . nouvelle édition, publiée d'après les manuscrits de la Bibliothèque royale, par le comte Beugnot . . . Paris, J. Renouard, 1842. 2 v.

   Includes a biography of Philippe de Remi, sire de Beaumanoir.

1899–1900

67 Coutumes de Beauvaisis par Philippe de Remi, sire de Beaumanoir; texte critique . . . par Am. Salmon . . . Paris, A. Picard et fils, 1899–1900. 2 v.

   Contains a brief biography of Philippe de Remi, sire de Beaumanoir, and a description of the extant manuscript of this coutume.

1903

68 La coutume du comté de Clermont-en-Beauvaisis de 1496, par Georges Testaud. Paris, Librairie de la Société du recueil Gal des lois et des arrêts, 1903. 107 p.

1970–74

69 Coutumes de Beauvaisis par Philippe de Remi, sire de Beaumanoir. Texte critique publié avec un introduction . . . par Am. Salmon. Paris, A. et J. Picard, 1970–74. 3 v.

Berry

The general coutume of Berry applied to that part of the region not ruled by the coutumes of Montargis, Blois, or Touraine.[14] The most ancient coutumier of Berry was that published by Gaspard Thaumas de la Thaumassière in his *Anciennes et Nouvelles Coutumes locales* under the title *Les Coutumes de la ville et septaine de Bourges, le Dun-le-Roy et du Pays de Berry.* This was a strictly private ancienne coutume for use in Bourges and its suburbs;[15] approximately one hundred chapters date from 1312, and most of the later chapters from 1380 to 1433.[16] *See also* coutume of Bourges.

In Bourges, the chief city of Berry, David Chambellan, lieutenant general of the bailli of Berry, with the cooperation of the officers and practicing lawyers of the bailliage, in 1449 undertook a compilation of the coutumes of Bourges entitled *Style du Palais Royal de Bourges avec les coutumes dudit lieu.* Charles VII approved this compilation through letters patent given at Tours on March 2, 1450 (O.S.).[17]

At the request of his sister, the duchess of Berry, Francis I on March 25, 1528, ordered a compilation of the coutume of Berry. President Pierre Lizet and parlement counselor Pierre Mathé proceeded with the compilation of the coutume in response to the royal letters, but difficulties delayed completion for some years. Finally, however, on June 8, 1540, the *Coutumes générales des pays et duché de Berry* were settled by an act of parlement.[18] The coutume of Berry, not published until 1679 by La Thaumassière,[19] is permeated with the spirit of Roman law.[20]

1509

70 Consuetudines inclite ciuitatis & septene Biturigũ per egregiũ virũ magistrã Nicolaũ boerij . . . nouiter editis. Lyons, 1509. 156 l.

Place of publication identified by the publisher's device of Symon Vincent.

1529

71 Consvetvdines generales Bituriceñ. Turoneñ. ac Aurelianeñ . . . Nicolao Boerij . . . Ioanne Sainson . . . ac Pyrro Englebermeo . . . elaborato . . . Parisijs, apud Frãciscũ Regnault, 1529. 379 l.

1531

72 Consuetudines inclite ciuitatis & septene Biturigum per . . . Nicolaum boerij . . . Parisijs, Col. Iehan Petit, 1531. 136 l.

1543

73 Consvetvdines Bituricẽses . . . à Domino Nicolao Boerio . . . Aurelianenses . . . Pyrrho Englebermeo . . . Turonenses . . . Ioanne Sainson . . . Parisiis à Galeoto Pratensi . . . 1543. 333 l.

1547

74 Conenta: Bitvrigvm consvetvdines, a Nicolao Boerio . . . Aurelianorum item consuetudines, à Pyrrho Englebermeo . . . Turonum item consuetudines, à Ioanne Sainson . . . Parisiis, Apud Oudoënum Paruum, 1547. 3471.

1579

75 Covstvmes generales des Pays et Duché de Berry. Auec les annotations de Gabriel

Labbé . . . Bovrges, Ambrois Brillard, 1579. 755 p.

1598

76 Consvetvdines infrascriptarvm civitatvm & prouinciarum Galliae. Bitvricensis, Nicolai Boerii. Avrelianensis, Pyrrhi Englebermei. Tvronensis, Ioan, Sainsonii. Lvcvlentiss commentariis . . . Dionysio Gothofredo . . . Francofvrti, Nicolai Bassaei, 1598. 147 p., 143 l., 245 p.

1607

77 Les covstvmes generales des pays et dvché de Berry. Avec les annotations de Gabriel Labbé . . . 2. ed., reu. & augm. Paris, Nicolas Bvon, 1607. 699 p.

1691

78 Questions et responses sur les coutumes de Berry . . . par Gaspard Thaumas de la Thaumassiere . . . 2. ed., rev. & augm. par l'Autheur. Bourges, François Toubeau, 1691. 638 p.

1691

79 J. Migeonis liber singularis defensarum quaestionum in legesbiturigum municipales. Avarici Biturigum, Francisci Toubeau, 1691. 40 p.
    See also Auvergne, no. 55 (1695).

1701

80 Nouveaux commentaires sur les coutumes generales des pays et duché de Berri par Gaspard Thaumas de la Thaumassiere . . . Nouvelle edition. Revue, corrigée et avgmentée par l'avtevr . . . Traité dv Franc-Alev de Berri . . . Bourges, Jean Jacques Cristo, 1701. 722, 51 p.

1744

81 Decisions sur les coutumes de Berry. Par Gaspard Thaumas de la Thaumassiere . . . Nouv. ed. augm. de notes. Bourges, Chez la veuve de Jacques Boyer, 1744. 726 p.

1750

82 Nouveaux commentaires sur les coutumes generales . . . de Berri par Gaspard Thaumas de la Thaumassiere . . . Burges, Cristo, 1750. 722, 51 p.

1915

83 Thaumas de la Thaumassière, commentateur des coutumes de Berry, par E. Mallet . . . Paris Edouard Duchemin, 1915. 452 p.

Includes history of the coutume of Berry and biographical sketches of those who have written commentaries on it.

1916
84 Le "pays" de Berry et le "détroit" de sa coutume, par Emile Chénon . . . Paris, Société du Recueil Sirey, 1916. 192 p.

Microfilm: 1607, 1615, 1624, 1667, 1673, 1691.

Blois

In 1523 President Roger Barme, with the assistance of Jean Prévot, counselor to the parlement, published the coutume of Blois. When Barme died before signing the procès-verbaux he had just finished putting in order, the parlement entrusted the new president, Antoine le Viste, with responsibility for completing this formality.[21]

1677
85 Dionysii Pontani in consvetvdines Blesenses commentariorvm . . . ex ms. codice Bibliothecae Seguierianae. Accedunt Notae Caroli Molinaei & rerum & verborum index amplissimus. Parisiis, I. Guignard, 1677. 2 v. in 1.
　　Text of the coutume in French.

1777
86 Coutumes générales du pays et comté de Blois . . . par Fourré . . . Blois, J. P. J. Masson, 1777. 2 v. in 1.

Microfilm: 1556, 1622, 1677, 1745, 1777.

Bourbonnais

Upon receiving permission from Louis XII on March 26, 1493, Pierre II, duke of Bourbonnais and Auvergne, count of Clermont, chose commissioners to compile the ancienne coutume of Bourbonnais.[22] On the orders of the king, commissioners de Besançon and Thibaut Baillet, president of the parlement of Paris, went to the city of Moulins, where they published the coutume of Bourbonnais on September 19, 1500.

Since this compilation was found to be incomplete, Anne of France, duchess of Bourbonnais, and her son-in-law Charles, duke of Bourbonnais, obtained new letters in 1520 from Francis I for the compilation and publication of a new coutume of Bourbonnais and the county of Marche. The king commissioned Roger Barme, president, and

Nicole Brachet, counselor to the parlement, to proceed. This new coutume was confirmed on March 13, 1521.[23]

1550
87 Ioannis Paponis Crozetii Forensis . . . In Bvrbonias consvetvdines commentaria. Lvgdvni, Apud Ioan Tornaesivm, 1550. 490 p.

1574
88 Le covstvmier dv pays et dvché de Bovrbonnois, avec le proces verbal. Corrigé & annoté . . . par Charles du Molin. Lyon, B. Vincent, 1574. 303 p.

1693
89 Coutumes generales du pays et duché de Bourbonnois . . . Notes de Charles du Moulin. Moulins, Claude Vernoy, 1693. 433 p.
　　See also Auvergne, no. 55 (1695), and general coutumes of France, no. 30 (1699).

1732
90 Coutumes generales et locales du païs et duché de Bourbonnois, avec le commentaire . . . a quoi on a joint les notes de Charles Dumoulin, les décisions tirées des commentaires imprimes de Jean Papon, Jean Duret, Jacques Potier . . . Par Messire Matthieu Auroux Des Pommiers . . . Paris, Paulus-Du-Mesnil, 1732. 2 v. in 1.

1732
91 Coutumes generales et locales du païs et duché de Bourbonnois . . . Par Matthieu Auroux des Pommiers. Paris, Osmont, 1732. 2 v. in 1.

1732
92 Coutumes générales et locales du païs et duché de Bourbonnois . . . à quoi on a joint les notes de Charles Dumoulin, les décisions tirées des commentaires imprimez de Jean Papon, Jean Duret, Jacques Potier . . . Par Matthieu Auroux Des Pommiers. Paris, Le Breton, 1732. 2 v. in 1.

1741
93 Additions au Nouveau commentaire de la coutume de Bourbonnois, par Matthieu Auroux des Pommiers . . . Paris, Le Breton, 1741. 2 v. in 1.

1780
94 Coutumes générales et locales du pays et duché de Bourbonnois . . . A quoi on a joint les

notes de Charles Dumoulin, les décisions tirées des commentaires imprimés de Jean Papon, Jean Duret, Jacques Potier . . . par Matthieu Auroux Des Pommiers. Riom, M. Dégoutte, 1780. 2 v. in 1.

Microfilm: 1573, 1754, 1780.

Bourges

The *Anciennes Coutumes de la ville et septaine de Bourges* were drawn up by the bailli of Berry; the same man also carried out the 1481 orders of Louis XI to codify the coutume of Mehun-sur-Yèvre. It was on this ancienne coutume of Bourges that the earliest commentator on coutumes, Nicolas de Bohier, president of the parlement of Bordeaux, wrote in 1508, a little more than thirty years before the redaction of the new coutume of Berry,[24] passed by parlement on June 8, 1540. *See also* coutume of Berry.

Chartres

The coutume of the bailliage of Chartres was published for the first time in 1508.[25]

1604
95 Les covstvmes dv dvché et bailliage de Chartres . . . avec les commentaires . . . de feu Charles dv Movlin, feu Gilles Tvlove . . . Nicolas Frerot . . . Paris, François Hvby, 1604. 128 p.

1630
96 Les covstvmes dv dvché et bailliage de Chartres . . . Avec les notes & apostyles de I. Covart . . . Paris, Denys Moreav, 1630. 590 p.

1679
97 Les trois coustumes voisines de Chasteavneuf, Chartres, et Drevx. Auec les notes de Ch. Dv Movlin . . . Chartres, la veuve Clousier, 1679. 3 v. in 1.

1687
98 Coutumes du duché, bailliage et siege presidial de Chartres . . . commentées par J. Couart . . . 2. éd. Augm. de notes de C. du Molin . . . Chartres, d'Estienne Massot, 1687. 592 p.

1714
99 Nouveau commentaire sur la coutume de Chartres, par Pierre de Merville. Paris, Henri Charpentier et Noel Pissot, 1714. 417 p.

Microfilm: 1560, 1714.

Clermont-en-Beauvaisis
See coutume of Beauvaisis.

Etampes

Etampes, originally under the prévôté of Paris, was later established as a bailliage with a coutume of its own. The coutume of Etampes was codified in response to royal letters of August 19, 1556. The commissioners were President Christofle de Thou, counselor to the parlement Barthélemy Faye, and lawyer to the king, Jacques Bourdin.[26]

1720
100 Coutume des baillage et prevosté du duché d'Estampes . . . commentées. Ouvrage posthumé de Marc-Antoine Lamy . . . Paris, Henry Charpentier, 1720. 544 p.

Loir-et-Cher

1888
101 Recueil des usages locaux du département de Loir-et-Cher, classés dans un ordre méthodique, par L. Leguay . . . Paris, Noizette, 1888. 262 p.

Lorris

Except for certain places covered by the coutume of Melun, after 1494 all of the Gâtinais was ruled by the coutume of Montargis, known as the coutume of Gâtinais or more generally as the coutume of Lorris, a neighboring town.[27]

In the first half of the twelfth century, the parish of Lorris had already obtained a charter of privileges from King Louis VI. A charter of franchise was given to the inhabitants of Lorris by Louis VII in 1155, and Philip II Augustus accorded a new confirmation in 1187.[28] The coutume of Lorris, which was renowned because of these franchises and privileges, was adopted very rapidly throughout not only the Gâtinais, but also in the Beauce and in Sologne.[29] The privileges of Lorris were renewed twice: first in 1448, under Charles VII, and later in 1625, under Louis XIII.[30]

On January 28, 1494 (N.S.), Charles VIII sent letters patent to the bailli of Montargis and to other baillis of the realm, reminding them of Charles VII's ordinance of 1454 and ordering them to draw up the coutumes of their regions by the following April 1. In response, on March 10 of that year, the bailli of Montargis ordered churchmen, nobles, officials, counselors, lawyers, citizens, and residents of the cities and places listed in the letters to come to Montargis on April 14 to draw up the coutume in writing. This redaction was completed April 24, 1494, but it was not officially published.

In 1498, when Louis XII came to the throne, the duchy of Orléans was reunited with the crown. On September 18, 1509, Louis XII issued letters patent ordering the redaction of the coutumes of the bailliage of Orléans. This coutume was published on October 22 under the title *Les Coutumes du bailliage et prévosté d'Orléans et ressors d'iceux, lesquelles d'ancienneté ont esté vulgairement appellées les coutumes de Lorris* (*see* no. 124).[31]

Representatives of Montargis and other neighboring places had been called together for the drafting of this 1509 coutume of Orléans, but they did not attend. There was, in fact, a rivalry between the bailliages of Orléans and of Montargis; each claimed the right to draw up the coutume for the region to the exclusion of the other. In 1530, the bailliage of Montargis obtained from Francis I letters patent ordering the commissioners to review the coutume drafted in Montargis in 1494 and then to publish it. After some protests from Orléans and Montargis, the new coutume was published in 1531. The rivalry between Orléans and Montargis appears to have been of little consequence, because the three compilations—Lorris Montargis in 1494, Lorris Orléans in 1509, and Lorris Montargis in 1531—hardly differ from one another. Those of 1494 and 1531 are generally known under the name of "Lorris" or "Montargis"; that of 1509 forms the true coutume of Orléans.[32] For more information, *see* coutume of Orléans.

1608
102 Les privileges, franchises, et libertez des bourgeois & habitans de la ville & faux-bourges de Montargis le Franc . . . Paris, Pierre Chevalier, 1608. 69 p.

1617
103 Les covstvmes anciennes de Lorris, des bailliages et prevosté de Montargis Le Franc . . . Par Antoine Lhoste . . . Charles dv Moulin. Paris, Thomas Blaise, 1617. 324 p.

1629
104 Les covstvmes anciennes de Lorris, des bailliage et prevosté de Montargis Le Franc . . . Commentees par Antoine Lhoste . . . avec les notes de Charles Du Moulin . . . Paris, Chez la veufue Gvillemot, 1629. 722 p.

1758
105 Coutumes de Lorris-Montargis . . . Commentées par Lhoste . . . avec les notes de Du Moulin. Nouv. ed., rev., cor. & augm. des Observations de Le Page . . . des coutumes de Paris, Orleans, Troyes & Auxerre . . . par Durand . . . Montargis, J. Bobin, 1758. 2 v.

1771
106 Coutumes de Lorris-Montargis . . . Commentées par Lhoste. Avec les notes de Moulin. Augm. des observations de Le Page, & de la conférence des coutumes de Paris, Orléans, Troies & Auxerre, par Durand. Nouv. éd. Montargis, Veuve J. Bobin, 1771. 2 v.

1885
107 . . . Coutumes de Lorris, publiées d'après le registre original du Parlement de Paris, par Ad. Tardif . . . Paris, A. Picard, 1885. 78 p.

Lists different editions of the coutumes of Lorris and reproduces the 1531 coutume by André Guillard, lieutenant-general, and others.

Microfilm: 1597, 1758.

Mantes

Mantes received a confirmation of certain privileges from Philip Augustus in 1201 and 1202.[33] Like that of Etampes, the coutume of the county and bailliage of Mantes was under the general jurisdiction of the coutume of Paris, and its object was to derogate some of the provisions of the coutume of Paris. The coutumes of Mantes and Etampes were compiled in response to letters patent of August 19, 1556, and were prepared by the same commissioners—de Thou, Faye, and Bourdin.[34]

1558
108 Covstvmes dv comté et bailliage de Mante & Meullant . . . par nous Christophle de

Thou, president, Barthelemy Faye et Iaques Viole. Paris, I. Dallier, 1558. 51 p.

Marche

Letters from Francis I of August 7, 1520, requested by the duchess of Bourbonnais, countess of Marche, ordered the publication of the coutume of Marche. Several collections of these coutumes had already been prepared.[35] *See also* Auvergne, no. 55 (1695).

1744
109 Coutumes de la province et comté pairie de la Marche . . . Avec des observations . . . par Couturier de Fournoue. Clermont-Ferrand, P. Viallanes, 1744. 308 p.

Meaux

The coutume of Meaux was published in 1509.[36] *See also* general coutumes of France, no. 1 (1517).

1682
110 Coustumes du bailliage de Meaux . . . avec les notes de C. du Moulin. 2. éd. . . . Par I. Champy. Paris, N. Pepingue, 1682. 469 p.

1683
111 Commentaire sur les coutumes generales du bailliage de Meaux. Avec des notes sur la coutume de Paris et une conference des deux coutumes . . . par Jean Bobé. Paris, 1683. 484 p.

Melun

The coutume of Melun was first codified in 1494, but it was, like that of Sens, not published until 1506. Henry II, in letters of February 12, 1558, objected to some sections of the coutume of Melun which were considered unreasonable. Consequently, the commissioners were directed to draft a new coutume. Although the death of Henry II interrupted this project, it was renewed by Francis II on July 24, 1559. The new coutume of Melun was published in 1560.[37] *See also* general coutumes of France, no. 1 (1517), and Mantes, no. 108 (1558).

1768
112 Coutume du bailliage de Melun . . . Avec des observations nouvelles . . . par Louis-Alphonse Sevenet. Sens, P.H. Tarbé, 1768. 476 p.

1777
113 Coutume du bailliage de Melun . . . Par Louis-Alphonse Sevenet . . . Paris, Gogué, 1777. 476 p.

Montargis
See coutume of Lorris.

Montfort-l'Amaury

Like that of Etampes, the coutume of the county of Montfort-l'Amaury was in the general jurisdiction of the coutume of Paris, and its object, in part, was to derogate that of Paris. It was compiled as a result of the same letters of August 19, 1556, and prepared by the same commissioners—de Thou, Faye, and Bourdin—as the coutumes of Etampes, Mantes, Meulan, and Vermandois.[38]

1693
114 Coutumes du comté et bailliage de Montfort-Lamaulry, Gambais, Neauphle-Le-Chastel, Saint-Liger en Yveline . . . par Claude Thourette . . . Paris, Jerosme Bobin, 1693. 478 p.

1731
115 Coutumes du comté et bailliage de Montfort-Lamaulry, Gambais, Neauphle-Le-Chastel, Saint-Liger en Yveline . . . Avec le commentaire de Claude Thourette . . . Paris, Jacques Clousier, 1731. 600 p.

Nivernais

The coutume of Nivernais was compiled, without the participation of the king of France, by the authority of the duke of Brabant, count of Nevers in 1490.[39] A second compilation was ordered by letters from Charles VIII and Louis XII. These first two coutumes were never issued in due form, and inquests by turbe were continued as though no official text existed. To end this situation, royal letters ordered a definitive draft of the coutume of Nivernais. In 1534 the coutume was published by counselors to the parlement, Louis

Rouillard and Guillaume Bourgoin, who were commissioned by the king at the request of the countess of Nivernais.

The coutume of Nivernais is unquestionably one of the most curious of the ancient French laws. Borrowing only rarely from Roman law, it maintained its French characteristics; some of its institutions are found in Nivernais alone.[40]

1605

116 Les covstvmes dv pays et dvché de Nivernois, avec les annotations et commentaires de Gvy Coqville. Paris, A. L'Angelier, 1605. 964 p.

1610

117 Covstvmes dv pays et dvché de Nivernois. Avec les annotations et commentaires de Gvy Coqville, sieur de Romenay. Paris, A. L'Angelier, 1610. 964 p.

1625

118 Les covstvmes dv pays et dvché de Nivernois. Avec les annotations et commentaires de Gvy Coqville . . . 3. éd. Paris, Clavde Cramoisy, 1625. 964 p.

1634

119 Les covstvmes dv pays et dvché de Nivernois. Avec les annotations et commentaires de Gvy Coqville . . . 4. éd. . . . Paris, Gvillavme Loyson, 1634. 964 p.

1635

120 Les covstvmes dv pays et dvché de Nivernois. Avec les annotations et commentaires de Gvy Coqville . . . 4. éd. . . . Paris, G. Loyson, 1635. 964 p.

1646

121 Les oeuvres de Gvy Coqville . . . contenant la coutume de Niuernois . . . Avec les instivtes covstvmiers de France, par A. Loysel . . . Paris, Henry le Gras, 1646. 3 v. in 1.
    See also Auvergne, no. 55 (1695).

1772

122 Coutumes du pays et duché de Nivernois . . . arrêts de commutation des Bordelages en la ville & fauxbourgs de Nevers. Nevers, P. Louis le Febvre, 1772. 334 p.

1864

123 La coutume de Nivernais, accompagnée d'extraits du Commentaire de cette coutume par

Guy Coquille . . . Nouvelle éd. . . . par Dupin . . . Paris, H. Plon, 1864. 524 p.

Microfilm: 1605, 1646.

Orléans

The two most important monuments of the medieval law of the Orléanais are the *Livre de jostice et de plet,* written between 1254 and 1260, and the *Etablissements de Saint Louis,* ca. 1273. In spite of its name, the *Etablissements de Saint Louis* cannot be directly linked to that king. Chapters 10 to 175 in Book One were borrowed from the old coutume of Anjou and Maine, and Book Two appears to have been borrowed from an ancient coutumier containing the usages of the Orléanais.[41]

In 1498, when Louis XII came to the throne, the duchy of Orléans was united with the crown. On September 18, 1509, Louis XII issued letters patent ordering the redaction of the coutumes of the bailliage of Orléans. This coutume was published on October 22, under the title *Les Coutumes du bailliage et prévosté d'Orleans et ressors d'iceux, lesquelles d'ancienneté ont esté vulgairement appellées les coutumes de Lorris* (no. 124).[42] It was published by two commissioners—Etienne Buynard, counselor to parlement, and Guillaume Roiger, attorney general. In force throughout the duchy of Orléans, it appears to have extended even into the Blaisois. The coutume of Orléans, corrected and reformed in 1583 in response to letters patent from Henry III, was closely associated with the coutumes of Lorris and Montargis.[43] For more information about the history of the coutume of Orléans, *see* coutume of Lorris.

1509

124 Les coustumes des bailliage & preuoste dorleãs . . . vulgairemẽt appelles Les coustumes de Lorryz . . . Paris, Jean Petit, ca. 1509. n. p.

1517 (i.e. 1509)

125 Commentarius in Aurelianas consuetudines. Aureliae, in aedibus Iacobi Hoys, 1517 [i.e. 1509] 106 p.
    With a commentary by Jean Pyrrhus d'Angleberme.
    See also general coutumes of France, no. 1 (1517), and Berry, no. 71 (1529), no. 72 (1531), no. 73 (1543), no. 74 (1547).

1583

126 Covstvmes des duché, bailliage, prevosté d'Orleans . . . mises & redigees par escrit . . . Par Achilles de Harlay [et al.] Orleans, Satvrny Hottot, 1583. 84, 40 l.

See also Berry, no. 76 (1598) and no. 77 (1607).

1609

127 Les covstvmes des dvchez, bailliages et prevosté d'Orleans . . . avec commentaires . . . par Iean Dvret. Paris, N. Bvon, 1609. 959 p.

1673

128 Coutumes des duché, bailliage, prevosté d'Orleans . . . Commentées par Jacques Delalande . . . Orleans, F. Hotot, 1673. 584 p.

1704–5

129 Coutume d'Orleans, commentée par Delalande. 2. éd., augm. . . . des notes de Gyves . . . Rev., corr., & mise en ordre par Philippe Auguste Perreaux. Orleans, J. Borde, 1704–5. 2 v.

First edition published in 1673; see no. 128 (1673).

1740

130 Coutumes des duché, bailliage, et prevosté d'Orleans, avec les notes de Henry Fornier . . . ; les notes de Dumoulin sur l'ancienne coutume d'Orleans . . . On y a joint . . . l'éloge de Delalande, & des observations sur son commentaire. Orleans, F. Rouzeau, 1740. 2 v.

See also Lorris, no. 105 (1758).

1760

131 Coutumes des duché, bailliage et prévôté d'Orleans . . . Orleans, J. Rouzeau-Montaut, 1760. 3 v. in 2.

Edited by R. J. Pothier.

See also Lorris, no. 106 (1771).

1772

132 Coutumes des duché, bailliage et prévôté d'Orleans . . . Le texte est accompagné de notes. Par Pothier. Paris, Debure Pere & Orléans, la Veuve Rouzeau-Montaut, 1772. 892 p.

1776

133 Coutumes des duché, bailliage et prévôté d'Orleans . . . par Pothier. Paris, Frères De-

bure; Orléans, la Veuve Rouzeau-Montaut, 1776. 2 v.

1780

134 Coutumes des duché, bailliage et prévôté d'Orléans . . . Le texte est accompagné de notes par Pothier. Nouvelle Edition. Paris, Debure l'aîné & Orléans, la Veuve Rouzeau-Montaut, 1780. 892 p.

Microfilm: 1609, 1673, 1702, 1704–5.

Paris

The ancienne coutume of Paris was the most important French coutume. It was sometimes called the coutume of the country of France because the parlement applied it to almost all of the ancient royal domain before the annexations of 1203. The ancienne coutume was mentioned in several texts, including a decretal of Celestin III in 1195. In 1212, Simon de Montfort modeled the feudal regime in the Albigeois after the coutume of Paris. This ancienne coutume was never compiled in writing.[44]

The coutume of Paris was codified quite late. The most important source of the coutume was furnished by a private compilation of the end of the fourteenth century known as the *Grand Coutumier de France*. Letters of January 21, 1510, from Louis XII commissioned the magistrates of the parlement to enact the coutume. Preliminary drafts were prepared by commissioners chosen from among lawyers and legal practitioners. The Trois Etats were then convened and the articles were discussed from March 8 to April 1, 1510, under the presidency of Thibaut Baillet, counselor to the king and president of the parlement. This draft of the coutume of Paris did not remain in force for long, however. It was reformed in 1580.

The coutume of Paris was truly original in several respects. It showed very little influence of Roman law and even less of canon law. The compilers tried to give the coutume, as far as possible, a national character. This was especially true of the great commission directed by President de Thou at the time of the reform of the coutume in 1580.[45]

1513

135 Les coustumes generalles de la preuoste et vicomte de Paris. Paris, Guillaume Eustace [et] Iehan Petit [1513]. 58 l.

Printer's device.

See also Normandy, no. 266 (1513), and general coutumes of France, no. 1 (1517).

1539–58

136 Prima [-secvnda] pars commentariorum in consvetvdines parisienses, authore Carolo Molendineo . . . Parisiis, apud Poncentum le Preux, 1539–58. 2 v. in 1.
See also Berry, no. 73 (1543).

1572

137 Prima [-secvnda] pars commentariorvm in consvetvdines parisienses, avthore Carolo Molendineo . . . Parisiis, Ioannes le Preux, 1572. 2 v. in 1 (v. 2, 1564).

1580

138 Covstvmes de la prevoste et vicomte de Paris . . . Paris, I. Dupuis, 1580. 113 l.

1581

139 Covstvmes de la prevoste et vicomte de Paris . . . par nous Chrestofle de Thou . . . Claude Anjorrant, Mathieu Chartier, Iaques Viole & Pierre de Longueil . . . Paris, Iaques du Puis, 1581. 49 l.

1598

140 Covstvme de la ville, prevosté et vicomté de Paris . . . Avec les commentaires de L. Charondas Le Caron . . . 2. éd. . . . Paris, P. L'Hvillier & I. Mettayer, 1598. 2 v. in 1.

1602

141 Covstvme de la ville, prevosté et vicomté de Paris . . . Auec les commentaires de L. Charondas Le Caron . . . 3. éd. . . . Paris, P. L'Hvillier & I. Mettayer, 1602. 287 l.

1603

142 De civilibvs Parisiorvm moribvs ac institvtis, Libri III. Ad Henricvm. IIII . . . Secvnda editio. Renati Choppini. Parisiis, apud Michaelem Sonnivm, 1603. 597, 162 p.

1605

143 Covstvme de la ville, prevosté et vicomté de Paris . . . par L. Charondas le Caron. 4. ed. Paris, Nicolas dv Possé, 1605. 222 l.

1614

144 Covstvme de la ville, prevosté et vicomté de Paris . . . auec les commentaires de L. Charondas Le Caron, reueus, corr., & augm. . . . 5. et derniere edition. Paris,

Pierre Chevalier, 1614. 620 p.
See also Beauvaisis, no. 64 (1615).

1618

145 Covstvme de la ville, prevosté et vicomté de Paris . . . Par Iean Tronçon. Paris, R. Foüet, 1618. 579 p.

1619

146 Texte des covstvmes de la prevosté et vicomté de Paris . . . 5. éd. . . . Paris, A. Bacot, 1619. 234 p.

1624

147 De civilibvs Parisiorvm moribvs ac institvtis. Libri III. Ad Henricvm IV . . . Editio vltima. Renati Choppini. Parisiis, Michaelem Sonnivm, 1624. 549 p.

1627

148 Covstvmes de la prevosté et vicomté de Paris. 2. ed. . . . Par I. Tovrnet . . . Paris, G. Alliot, 1627. 610 p.

1634

149 Commentaire svr les covstvmes de la prevosté et vicomté de Paris . . . composé en latin par René Choppin . . . Paris, Estienne Richer, 1634. 320 p.
See also Anjou, no. 204 (1651).

1652

150 Conference de la covstvme de Paris avec les avtres covstvmes de France . . . auec les notes de C. Dv Movlin. Paris, Pierre Lamy, 1652. 648 p.
"Plus une recherche . . . par G. Fortin."
See also Maine, no. 258 (1657).

1658

151 Commentaire svr la covstvme de la prevosté et vicomté de Paris, fait par Ivlien Brodeav . . . Paris, D. Bechet et Lovis Billaine, 1658. 2 v.

1662

152 Commentaire svr les covstvmes de la prevosté et vicomté de Paris, divisé en trois livres, composé en latin par René Choppin . . . derniere edition . . . Paris, E. Covterot, 1662. 444 p.
Publisher's device on title page.
Translator's preface signed: Gabriel Michel de la Rochemaillet.

1665

153 Covstvmes de la prevosté et vicomté de Paris.
Avec les notes de C. Dv Molin, les observa-
tions de I. Tovrnet, Iacq. Ioly, & Ch.
Labbé . . . Derniere edition. Paris, André
Sovbron, 1665. 1000 p.

1667

154 Novveav recveil d'arrests et reglemens. Svr les
plvs belles qvestions de droit & de coustume . . . par F. Des-Maisons. Paris, G. de
Lvynes, 1667. 272 p.

1669

155 Covstvme de la prevosté et vicomté de Paris,
commentée par feu maistre Ivlien Bro-
deav . . . 2. ed. avgm. . . . Paris, D. Bechet,
1669. 2 v.
    Printer's mark on title page.

1669

156 Covstvme de la prevosté et vicomté de Paris,
commentée par feu Ivlien Brodeav. 2. ed.
avgm. . . . Paris, I. Gvignard, 1669. 2 v.

1678

157 Coustumes de la prevosté et vicomté de Paris,
Avec les notes de C. du Molin . . . Derniere
edition. Paris, Thomas Moette, 1678. 922 (i.e.
722) p.
    Table of places ruled by these coutumes.

1679

158 Nouveau commentaire sur la Coutume de la
prevosté et vicomté de la ville de Paris . . .
Par Claude de Ferriere . . . Paris, J. Cochart,
1679. 2 v. in 1.
    See also Meaux, no. 111 (1683), and Au-
vergne, no. 55 (1695).

1699

159 Traitez de Duplessis . . . sur la Coutume de
Paris. Avec des notes pour servir de preuves,
& des dissertations de Berroyer & de
Lauriere . . . Paris, Nicolas Gosselin, 1699.
904 p.

1700

160 La coûtume de la prevosté et vicomté de
Paris . . . par Pierre le Maistre. Paris, G. Cavelier, 1700. 576 p.

1708

161 Nouveau commentaire sur la coutume de la
prevosté de Paris par Claude de Fer-

riere . . . Nouvelle edition . . . Paris, la
veuve de Jean Cochart, 1708. 2 v.

1709

162 Traités de Duplessis . . . sur la coutume de
Paris. 3. éd. avec les notes de Berroyer & de
Lauriere. Paris, Nicolas Gosselin, 1709. 846,
136 p.

1714

163 Corps et compilation de tous les commentateurs . . . sur la coutume de Paris, par
Claude de Ferriere. 2 éd. revuë, corr. et augm.
par l'auteur et Claude Joseph de Ferriere, son
fils . . . enrichie . . . feu Le Camus. Paris,
Michel David, 1714. 4 v.

1714

164 Corps et compilation de tous les commentateurs . . . sur la coutume de Paris, par
Claude de Ferriere, 2 éd. revuë, corr. et
augm. par l'auteur et Claude Joseph de Ferriere, son fils . . . enrichie . . . feu Le
Camus. Paris, Nicolas Gosselin, 1714. 4 v.

1726

165 Nouveau commentaire sur la coutume de la
prevosté et vicomté de Paris, par Claude de
Ferriere. Nouv. éd. rev., corr. & augm. Paris,
Le Gras, 1726. 2 v.
    See also Chaumont-en-Bassigny, no. 445
(1733) and no. 446 (1733).

1740

166 Texte des coustumes de la prevosté et vicomté
de Paris . . . nouv. éd. Paris, Prault, pere,
1740. 162 p.

1741

167 Coutume de Paris . . . par Pierre le Maistre.
Nouv. éd. . . . par M. ***. Paris, Theodore
le Gras, 1741. 691 p.

1741

168 Coutume de Paris . . . par Pierre le Maistre. Nouv. éd. . . . par . . . M. ***. Paris,
Claude Jean-Baptiste Bauche, fils, 1741.
691 p.

1747

169 Le droit commun de la France et la Coutume
de Paris . . . Par François Bourjon . . .
Paris, Grangé, 1747. 2 v.

1754–

170 Traités de [Claude] Duplessis . . . sur la coutume de Paris. 5. éd. Avec des notes de Berroyer & de Lauriere. Paris, Jean de Nully, 1754– [vol. 1 only, 978 p.]
See also Lorris, no. 105 (1758).

1759

171 Actes de notoriété donnés au Châtelet de Paris . . . avec des notes, par J. B. Denisart . . . Paris, Savoye, 1759. 617 p.

1762

172 Nouveau commentaire sur la coutume de prevosté et vicomté de Paris. Par Claude de Ferriere . . . Nouv. éd., rev., corr. & augm. Par Sauvan d'Aramon . . . Paris, Guillyn, 1762. 2 v.
Vol. 2 has imprint: Paris, Chez Dufour.

1764

173 Texte des coutumes de la prevosté et vicomté de Paris, avec des notes . . . par Claude de Ferriere. Paris, Compagnie des Libraires, 1764. 284 p.

1770

174 Le droit commun de la France, et la coutume de Paris . . . nouv. éd. . . . par François Bourjon . . . Paris, Grangé & Cellot, 1770. 2 v.
See also Lorris, no. 106 (1771).

1777

175 Texte des coutumes de la prévoté et vicomté de Paris; par Eusebe de Lauriere. Paris, Nyon, 1777. 2 v.

1779

176 Nouveau commentaire sur la coutume de la prévôté de Paris. Par Claude de Ferriere. Nouvelle edition, revue, corrigée & augmentée, par Sauvan d'Aramon. Lyon, J. Sulpice Grabit, 1779. 2 v.

1787

177 La Coutume de Paris mise en vers par G**. D** . . . 3. ed. Paris, de l'Imprimerie de Monsieur, 1787. 285 p.

1886

178 Essai sur l'ancienne coutume de Paris aux XIIIe et XIVe siècles. Par H. Buche. Paris, L. Larose et Forcel, 1886. 136 p.

1922–30

179 Histoire de la coutume de la prévôté et vicomté de Paris, par Olivier Martin . . . Paris, Ernest Leroux, 1922–30. 2 v. in 3.

1925

180 La coutume de Paris; trait d'union entre le droit romain et les législations modernes; six cours professés en mars 1925 à l'Université d'Utrecht par Olivier Martin . . . Paris, Recueil Sirey, 1925. 81 p.

Microfilm: 1539, 1603, 1605, 1613, 1618, 1625, 1634, 1643, 1650, 1652, 1660, 1664, 1665, 1666, 1669, 1678, 1691, 1698, 1708, 1714, 1742, 1770, 1777.

Perche

The coutume of the county and bailliage of Grand Perche included the seats of Mortagne, Bellême, and Nogent le Rotrou.[46] It was drawn up in response to special letters sent by the king to the duke of Alençon, count of Perche, in 1505.[47]

1571

181 Covstvmes des pays, comte et bailliage dv grand Perche . . . Paris, Iehan Dallier, 1571. 100 p.

1621

182 Covstvmes des pays, comté et bailliage dv grand Perche . . . Paris, Pierre Le-Mvr, 1621. 44, 39 p.

1737

183 Coustumes des pays, comté et bailliage du grand Perche . . . Nouv. ed. . . . Mortagne, Andre Bailly, 1737. 66 p.

Senlis

Senlis was conceded a charter by Louis VII in 1173.[48] The ancient jurisdiction of Senlis was ruled by three general coutumes—those of Senlis, Clermont-en-Beauvaisis, and Valois. These three coutumes were published in 1539 by commissioners André Guillard and Nicole Thibault.[49] *See also* Beauvaisis, no. 64 (1615).

1631

184 Les covstvmes generales de bailliages de Senlis, comté de Clermont en Beauuoisis, &

duché de Vallois. Derniere éd. commentée par Lavrent Bovchel. Paris, R. Bovtonné, 1631. 239, 160, 499 p.

1664
185 Les covstvmes dv bailliage de Senlis . . . Avec des remarqves particullieres . . . par Iean Marie Ricard . . . Paris, Iean Gvignard, le pere, 1664. 309 p.

1703
186 Coûtumes du bailliage de Senlis, et son ancien ressort; comprenant Senlis, Beauvais, Compiegne, Pointoise, Chaumont, Magny, Beaumont, Chambly, & Creil . . . Des commentaires de J. Marie Ricard, & Laurent Bouchel . . . Par De S. Leu . . . Paris, Maurice Villery, 1703. 541 p.

Microfilm: 1631, 1637, 1771.

Touraine

The history of the local legislation of the city of Tours is interesting. In 1181 Philip Augustus gave a charter to the inhabitants of Châteauneuf, but the administrators continued to ask for the status of commune. In 1356, as a defense against the English, Châteauneuf and Tours were united and enclosed within the same town walls. Officials elected to see to the construction of the fortifications took into their own hands all administration except justice, which was left to the royal bailli. This situation lasted until 1461. At that time, Louis XI confirmed for Tours some ancient municipal franchises, but the following year he gave the city the constitution of La Rochelle (the *Etablissements de Rouen*), which relieved the town of the expense of maintaining the fortifications.

The coutume of Touraine is similar to those of Anjou and Maine; until 1323, the three provinces had formed one sénéchaussée. The coutume was codified in 1460 in response to the edict issued by Charles VII in 1454.[50] In 1507, an assembly at Tours was charged with codifying, more completely than had been done before, the coutume of the region. This coutume was published in 1507 by Baillet and Burdelot.[51] A new coutume of Touraine was published in 1559 by Christofle de Thou, Barthélemy Faye, and Jacques Viole. This coutume was completely French in the sense that it was not influenced by Roman law.[52]

1507
187 Le coustumier de Touraine. Thibault Baillet et Jehan Burdelot. Paris, Anthoine Gerard, 1507. 120 l.

1528
188 Consuetudines totius presidatus seu Turoñensis . . . commento . . . Johannis Sainxon . . . Paris, Jacques Poussin, 1528. 232 l.
   See also Anjou, no. 204 (1651).

1654
189 Texte des covstvmes dv pays, dvché et bailliage de Touraine . . . Edition novvelle . . . Tovrs, Vrbain Nion, 1654. 454 p.

1661
190 Covstvmes dv dvché et bailliage de tovraine . . . avec les annotations de Estienne Pallv . . . Tovrs, E. La Tovr, 1661. 775 p.

1761
191 Abregé du Commentaire de la Coutume de Touraine . . . par Jacquet. Auxerre, Fournier; Paris, Knapen, 1761. 2 v.

Tours
See coutume of Touraine. *See also* Berry, no. 71 (1529), no. 73 (1543), no. 74 (1547), and no. 76 (1598).

Visit to a sickroom, folio 77. This miniature probably portrays the procedure followed when a defendant is too ill to appear in court. Among other steps, a bailiff, accompanied by four knights or eight honest men above suspicion, must visit the sick person to verify his illness. "Langour prolongue de plet. Quant trois essoÿnes sont faictes len doit comander que la personne de cil qui a este essoine doit veue el lieu que li essongneur dirent quil gesoit malade et iour doit estre uns a celui qui a este essoine et a son adversaire de le veoir. Et si doit li baillif aller ÿ et ÿ mener avec lui iiij chrĩs ou plus ou viij loyaulx homes q̂ ne soient pas souppeconeux qui viennent par semonce. . . . Se il veult iurer langour il iurera en ceste fourme. que il croit avoir telle maladie q'il na pas esperance de garir dedens ung an et ung iour li chevallier et li aultres qui sont presens a iurer la langour doivent venir aux premieres assises et recorder q̂ cil a iurer langour." (folios 81r to 82r)

Coutumes of the Western Region

To the west of the central region of France are the provinces of Normandy, Brittany, Maine, Anjou, the small county of Loudun, and the vast county of Poitou; also the regions of Aunis, Saintonge, and Angoumois. The customary laws of this western region contain many borrowings from English institutions, and, as may be expected, the reciprocal influence of English and French legal concepts is particularly strong in Normandy.[53]

Angers

1748
192 Recueil des priviléges de la ville et mairie d'Angers, rédigé par Robert . . . Angers, Louis-Charles Barriere, 1748. 2 v.

Angoumois

The coutume of Angoumois ruled all of the territory of that name and had many feudal characteristics. It was codified for the first time in 1514, with the official coutumes of Poitou and La Rochelle,[54] and published that year by Baillet and Barme.[55] There had been earlier usages written by jurisconsult Jean Faber (d. 1340), who taught Roman law at Montpellier and was a lawyer at Angoulème.[56]

1598
193 Exposition sommaire svr les covstvmes de la dvché et seneschavssée d'Angoumois. Par Pierre Gandillavd seigneur de Fonfroide. Paris, Michel Sonnivs, 1598. 294 p.

1633
194 Exposition sommaire sur les covstvmes de la dvché et seneschaussée d'Angoumois. Par Pierre Gandillavd . . . des notes de Du Moulin . . . Angovlesme, Clavde Rezé, 1633. 233 p.

1650
195 Les covstvmes dv pais et dvché d'Angoumois, avnis, et govvernement de la Rochelle, avec la comparison des devx covstvmes: Le commentaire . . . de Iean Vigier . . . Paris, Gervais Aliot, 1650. 550 p.

1720
196 Les coustumes du pais et duché d'Angoumois, aunis et gouvernement de la Rochelle. Avec les commentaires de Jean Vigier . . . 2 éd. . . . Jacques Vigier . . . François Vigier . . . Philippe Pigornet . . . Angouléme, Simon Rezé et Maurice Puinesge, 1720. 702 p.

1780–83
197 Coutume d'Angoumois, commentée et conférée avec le droit commun du royaume de France; par Etienne Souchet . . . Paris, Au Bureau de l'abonnement littéraire, 1780–83. 2 v.

Reflects the text of this coutume codified and deposited with the greffe (court record office) in 1588.

Anjou

Until 1442, Anjou and Maine were one sénéchaussée. Even after the separation, the two regions continued to be ruled by the same coutume, which was officially codified in 1462. Letters of April 12, 1506, however, ordered that the coutumes of Anjou and Maine be compiled separately and published; this was completed in 1508 by Baillet and Jean Lelièvre, counselors to the parlement, and Barme, lawyer to the king. Henry II in 1558 and Francis II in 1559 ordered a reform of the new coutumes codification but the reform was not carried out, and the coutumes of Anjou and Maine were never reformed after their original publication in 1508.[57] As a result, the laws of the regions were rich in ancient coutumiers and usages.[58] *See* coutume of Maine for more information.

1486 (incunabulum)
198 La premiere partie. Cy commencment les coustumes des pays daniou et du maine . . . 12 mai 1486.

1509(?)
199 Les coustumes du pays et duche Daniou auec le proces verbal publiees par Thibault baillet et Jehan le lieur . . . Paris, Dangiers [1509?] 136 p.

1530
200 Excellentissimi ivris interpretis, Frācisci Mingon . . . Commentaria in consuetudines ducatus Andegauensis . . . Parisiis, Ioanne Paruo, 1530. 261 p.
Printer's mark on title page and at end.

1605
201 Devx livres de la ivrisprvdence françoise, avec belles remarqves et decisions notables tirées des Loix Françoises & Romaines . . . Le tout rapporté sur chacun article de la coustume d'Anjou. Par Pierre Delommeav . . . Savmvr, Thomas Portav, 1605. 228, 409 p.

1611
202 Renati Choppini . . . De legibvs Andivm mvnicipalibvs libri III. Cum praeuio tractatu, De summis gallicarum consuetudinum regulis . . . 3. ed. Parisiis, apud L. Sonnium, 1611. 632, [70], 654, [79] p.
Printer's mark on title page.

1646
203 Observations, qvestions et responses sur avcvns articles de la Covstvme d'Aniov . . . Angers, P. Avril, 1646. 62 p.

1651
204 Covstvmes dv pays et dvché d'Aniov. Auec des notes sur chaque article seruans de confé-rence aux coûtumes du Maine, Paris, & Touraine . . . Par Pierre Tovraille . . . La Fleche, George Griveav, 1651. 576 p.
See also Maine, no. 258 (1657).

1698
205 Coûtumes du pays et duché d'Anjou . . . avec le commentaire de Gabriel Du Pineau . . . Auquel il a joint les notes de Charles Du Moulin . . . Paris, C. Osmont, 1698. 1301, 2911 p.

1725
206 Coustumes du pays et duché d'Anjou, confer-ées avec les coustumes voisines . . . avec le commentaire de Gabriel Dupineau . . . les notes de Charles du Moulin . . . nouvelle et derniere Edition . . . par Claude Pocquet de Livonniere . . . Paris, Jean Baptiste Coig-nard, 1725. 2 v.

1751
207 Coustume du pays et duché d'Anjou, con-ferée avec les coustumes voisines, Nouvelle edition . . . Angers, Louis-Charles Barriere, 1751. 558 p.
See also Maine, no. 261 (1778–79).

1783
208 Principes des coutumes d'Anjou et du Maine, Avec le Texte de ces deux Coutumes, qui for-mera le second Volume, Par Trottier . . . Angers, Mame, 1783. 2 v.

Brittany

The ancienne coutume of Brittany was primarily a book of civil and criminal procedure. It was cited publicly in 1341 before the court of Paris, but its precise date and the identity of its authors are sub-ject to debate.[59]

The coutume of Brittany was no less original than that of Normandy. It also adopted some prin-ciples of English law, especially in matters of the succession of certain fiefs, and was more affected by canonical law than any other region of France.

The last coutume to be codified during the reign of Francis I, it was published October 21–23, 1539, at Nantes, in response to letters patent of August 16 of the same year. The Etats of Brittany re-quested a new reform in 1575. Henry III named the Breton commissioners, who, in cooperation with commissioners from the Etats and ad-vised by the celebrated legal scholar Bertrand d'Argentré, compiled the final codification in 1580.[60]

1528
209 Coustumes establis/semens et ordonnances

du/pays & Duche de bretaigne . . . Ex car-racterib parrhisiis, 1528. 215 (i.e. 199) l.

1540

210 Covstvmes generalles des pays et dvche de Bretaigne . . . Rennes & Nantes, Philippes Bourgoignon, 1540. 94, 66 l.

1568

211 Coustumes generales du pais et dvche de Bretagne . . . Rennes, Julien du Clos, 1568. 615 p.

1585

212 Covstvmes generalles dv pays et dvché de Bretagne, reformées en l'an mil cinq cens quatre vingts par ordonnance du roy . . . auctore B. d'Argentré . . . Paris, I. Dupuys, 1585. 172 l.

1605

213 V. c. Bertrandi d'Argentré Rhedonensis provinciae praesidis, commentarii. Ad praecipvos ivris britannici titulos . . . Parisiis, N. Bvon, 1605. 240, 427, 156 p.

1608

214 V. C. Bertrandi d'Argentré . . . Commentarii in patrias Britonvm leges: sev (vt vvlgo . . .) . . . Parisiis, Nicolaum Buon, 1608. 2400 p.

1608

215 Covstvmes generales dv pays et dvché de Bretagne . . . V. C. Bertrandi d'Argentré Rhedonensis . . . Paris, Nicolas Buon, 1608. 119 p.

1614

216 V. c. B. d'Argentré, Redonensis provinciae praesidis, Commentarii in patrias Britonvm leges, seu Consuetudines generales antiquissimi ducatus Britanniae. In lvcem editi cvra et studio v. c. Caroli d'Argentré . . . Editio al-dera . . . Parisiis, Nicolai Bvon, 1614. 2460 p.

1617

217 Epitome ov abbregé des observations forenses . . . des coustumes, confirmées par Arrest du Parlement de Bretagne. Par Pierre Belordeav. Paris, Nicolas Bvon, 1617. 684 p.

1621

218 V. C. B. d'Argentré Redonensis provinciae praesidis, Commentarii in patrias Britonvm leges, seu consuetudines generales antiquissimi Ducatus Britanniae . . . Editio tertia emendatissima . . . Parisiis, Nicolai Bvon, 1621. 2471 p.

1621

219 Covstvmes generales dv pays et dvché de Bretagne . . . B. d'Argentré . . . Paris, Nicolas Buon, 1621. 119 p.

1622

220 Epitome ov Abbregé des observations forenses . . . des coustumes, & partie d'icelles confirmée par Arrest du Parlement de Bretagne. Par Pierre Belordeav . . . 2. éd. . . . Paris, Nicolas Bvon, 1622. 829 p.

1628

221 V. c. B. d'Argentré Redonensis provinciae praesidis, Commentarii, in patrias Britonvm leges, seu Consuetudines generales antiquissimi ducatus Britanniae. In lvcem editi cvra et studio v. c. Caroli d'Argentré . . . Ed. 4. . . . Parisiis, Nicolai Bvon, 1628. 1472 (i.e. 2472) l.

Author's portrait on verso of preliminary leaf.

1628

222 Covstvmes generales dv pays et dvché de Bretagne . . . B. d'Argentré. Paris, Nicolas Buon, 1628. 120 p.

1635

223 Les covstvmes generales des pays et dvché de Bretagne . . . par Pierre Belordeav . . . 3. éd. . . . Paris, Nicolas Bvon, 1635. 1033 p.

1640

224 V. c. B. d'Argentré, Rhedonensis provinciae praesidis, Commentarii in patrias Britonvm leges, seu Consuetudines generales antiqiss. ducatus Britanniae. In lvcem editi cura & studio v. c. Caroli d'Argentré . . . Ed. 5. . . . Parisiis, N. Bvon, 1640. 2288 p.

1640

225 Covstvmes generales dv pays et dvché de Bretagne . . . B. d'Argentré. Paris, Nicolas Bvon, 1640. 120 p.

1644

226 L'vsement dv domaine congeable de l'evesché et comté de Cornoaille, Commenté par Ivlien

Fvric . . . Auex l'vsement local de la Princi-
pauté de Leon, & Iurisdiction de Daoulas
. . . Paris, v. c. N. P. B. d'Argentré . . .
1644. 70 p.

1646
227 Commentarii in patrias britonvm leges, seu
consuetudines generales antiquiss. Ducatus
Britanniae . . . Parisiis, N. Bvon, 1646.
2288 p.

1646
228 Covstvmes generales dv pays et dvché de Bretagne . . . authore B. d'Argentré . . .
Paris, Nicolas Bvon, 1646. 120 p.

1651
229 Les covstvmes generales des pays et dvché de
Bretaigne . . . Rennes, Iean Vatar et Iean
Gaisne, 1651. 303 p.

1651
230 Les nobles covtvmes ov gvidon, stille et
vsances des marchands qvi mettent a la
mer . . . Rennes, Iean Vatar et Iean Gaisne,
1651. 112 p.

1655(?)
231 Covstvmes generales dv pays et dvché de Bretagne. Avec les paraphrase & brefue exposition literale & analogique sur icelle, par Pierre
Belordeav. Rennes, P. Garnier [1655?]
900 p.
    Title page is missing.

1660
232 Covstvmes generales dv pays et dvché de Bretagne . . . B. d'Argentré . . . 1580 . . .
Parisiis, Iacobvm d'Allin, 1660. 112 p.

1661
233 V. C. B. d'Argentré . . . Commentarii in patrias Britonvm leges, seu consuetudines generales antiquiss. Ducatus Britanniae . . .
Parisiis, Apud Iacobvm d'Allin, 1661. 2,
163 col.

1664
234 V. C. B. d'Argentré . . . Commentarii in patrias Britonum leges, seu Consuetudines
generales antiquiss . . . ducatus Britanniae
. . . Bruxellis, Franciscum Foppens, 1664.
2164 col.

1664
235 Coustumes generales du pays et duché de

Bretagne. Reformées en l'an 1580 . . . Am-
stelodami, Johannis Stammii, 1664. 64 p.

1694
236 Coutume de Bretagne, avec des observations
. . . Par messire René de La Bigotière . . .
Nouv. ed., rev., corr. & augm. Rennes, P.
Garnier, 1694. 555 p.

1702
237 Commentaires sur la Coutume de Bretagne,
ou, Institutions au droit françois par rapport
a la meme Coutume. Par messire René de la
Bigotierre . . . 2. éd. Rev. & augm. par
l'autheur. Rennes, La veuve de P. Garnier,
1702. 816 p.

1710
238 Coustume de Bretagne, avec les commentaires et observations . . . par Michel Sauvageau . . . Nantes, J. Mareschal, 1710- 2 v.
    Vol. 2 has title: La tres-ancienne coustume
de Bretagne, les annotations de l'an-
onime . . . Avec la conference des coustumes . . . Nantes, Jacques Mareschal, 1710.

1710
239 Observations pour la reformation de la coutume de Bretagne, avec un traité . . . Par
Michel Sauvageau. Nantes, J. Mareschal,
1710. 2 v.
    Vol. 2 has title: La tres-ancienne coustume
de Bretaigne, les annotations de l'ano-
nime . . . avec la conference des covstvmes
. . . Nantes, J. Mareschal, 1710.

1725
240 Coutume de Bretagne et usances particulieres
de quelques villes et territoires de la mesme
province . . . Préferences & l'autre des Pres-
criptions, par Monsieur ***. l ed. Nantes, N.
Verger, 1725. 585, 64, 26 p.

1734
241 Consultations et observations sur la coûtume
de Bretagne . . . par feu Pierre Hevin.
Rennes, G. Vatar, 1734. 720 p.

1737
242 Coûtumes de Bretagne, avec les commentaires et observations . . . par maître Michel
Sauvageau . . . Nouv. ed., augm. consider-
ablement. Rennes, J. Vatar, 1737. 623 p.
    "Traité des domaines congeables, a l'use-

ment . . . , composé & redigé par écrit par ecuyer F. de Rozmar."

1745–48

243 Coûtumes generales du païs et duché de Bretagne . . . avec . . . les notes de Pierre Hevin . . . Les arrests recueillis par le mesme auteur . . . l'Aitiologie de Bertrand d'Argentre . . . La traduction abregée de son Commentaire sur l'ancienne coûtume de Bretagne par H. E. Poullain de Belair . . . et les notes de Charles Du Moulin sur la même coûtume. Revû, corrigé & augmenté . . . avec les notes par A. M. Poullain Duparc . . . Rennes, G. Vatar, 1745–48. 3 v.

1759

244 La coutume et la jurisprudence coutumiere de Bretagne, dans leur ordre naturel, par A. M. Poullain du Parc. Rennes, G. Vatar, 1759. 372 p.

1771

245 Coutumes de Bretagne, avec les commentaires & observations . . . Par Michel Sauvageau . . . Nouv. éd., augm. . . . sur le texte de plusieurs articles de la coutume de cette province. Rennes, Remelein, 1771. 716 p.

> "Traité des domaines congéables, a l'usement . . . , composé & rédigé par écrit par ecuyer F. de Rozmar."

1778

246 La coutume et la jurisprudence coutumière de Bretagne, dans leur ordre naturel; par Poullain du Parc . . . 3. éd., rev., corr. & augm. Rennes, Veuve de F. Vatar, 1778. 448 p.

1896

247 La très ancienne coutume de Bretagne, avec les assises . . . suivies d'un recueil de textes divers antérieurs à 1491. Ed. critique . . . par Marcel Planiol . . . Rennes, J. Plihorn et L. Hervé, 1896. 566 p.

> Appendix: "Les manuscrits" and "Les anciennes éditions" of the coutume of Brittany.

Microfilm: 1570, 1584, 1693, 1710.

La Rochelle

This coutume applied in the country of Aunis and the Ile de Ré, south of Poitou.[61] Officially codi-fied and published by Baillet and Barme in 1514 at the end of the reign of Louis XII,[62] it conformed in many ways to the coutumes of Angoumois and Poitou.[63] Although orders to reform the coutume were issued by Henry II on February 12, 1558, and renewed by Francis II on July 24, 1559, these were never carried out.[64] *See also* Angoumois, no. 195 (1650) and no. 196 (1720).

1756

248 Nouveau commentaire sur la coutume de La Rochelle et du pays d'Aunis . . . Par René-Josué Valin . . . La Rochelle, René-Jacob Desbordes, 1756. 3 v.

1768

249 Nouveau commentaire sur la coutume de La Rochelle et du pays d'Aunis . . . Par René-Josué Valin . . . Nouv. éd., augm. . . . depuis la premiere édition. Par M. ***, avocat au Parlement . . . Paris, Vincent, 1768. 3 v.

Loudun

The coutume of Loudun was codified by order of Louis XII (d. 1515), but it was only published in 1518 by Charles de La Mothe, counselor to the king, in response to letters from Francis I.[65] It has never been revised.[66] The coutume of Loudun is in many ways analogous to the *Establissements de Saint-Louis* and the coutume of Tours.[67]

1517(?)

250 Coustumes du pays et seigneurie de Lodunoys. Poictiers, Bouchetz, freres [1517?] 71 l.

1612

251 Commentaires svr les covstvmes dv pays de Lovdvnois . . . par Pierre Le Provst. Savmvr, T. Portau, 1612. 595 p.

Maine

The coutume of Maine, like that of Anjou, was published in 1508 by Baillet and Jean Lelièvre, counselors to the parlement, and Barme, lawyer to the king. This coutume applied in the county of Maine, in the seats of Mans, Beaumont, Freisney, Ferté Bernard, Château du Loir, Mayenne, and the county of Laval.[68] For more information, *see* coutume of Anjou.

1509

252 Ce sont les coustumes du pays et conte du Maine publiees par Thibault et Jehan le lieure par commission et mandement du Roy. Paris, Gillet Couteau, 1509. 183 l.

1535

253 Le grāt coustumier du pays & Côte du Maine tres utile & prouffitable a tous practiciēs . . . [par] Guillaume le Rouille Dalēcon . . . Venundatur Parisijs in edibus Frācisci Regnault . . . 1535. 137 l.

1607

254 Les covstvmes du pays et conté du Maine. Nouuellement reueuës & corrigées et oultre les precedents impressions. Avec vne table tres amples . . . Mans, la vefue Hierome Olivier, 1607. 168 p.

1618

255 Les covstvmes dv pays et comté du Maine. Nouuellement reueuës & corrigées outre les precedentes impressions. Avec vne table tresamples . . . Mans, Gervais Olivier, 1618. 497 p.

1645

256 Les covstvmes dv païs et comté dv Maine. Avec les commentaires de Ivlien Bodreav . . . Paris, A. Alliot, 1645. 734 p.
See also Anjou, no. 204 (1651).

1655

257 Covtvmes dv pais et comté dv Maine. Avecques les notes de C. du Moulin. Reveuës, corr., & augm. . . . par Ivlien Bodreav. Derniere ed. Mans, H. Olivier, 1655. 310, 71 p.

1657

258 Remarques et notes sommaires svr la covtvme dv Maine . . . par Mathvrin Lövis . . . Mans, H. Olivier, 1657. 359, 16, 24, 20 p.

1658

259 Illvstrations et remarqves svr les covtvmes dv Maine. Reveuës, corrigées & augmentées de plusieurs décisions, sentences & arests. Par Maître Ivlien Bodreav . . . Mans, Hierôme Olivier, 1658. 2 v.

1728

260 Oeuvres de Duplessis . . . contenant un traité des matieres criminelles. Avec notes:

plusieurs traitéz sur la coutume du Maine . . . Paris, Nicolas Gosselin, 1728- [v. 2 only]

1778–79

261 Commentaire sur les coutumes du Maine et d'Anjou . . . Par Louis Olivier de Saint-Vast . . . Alençon, J. Z. Malassis le jeune, 1778–79. 4 v.
See also Anjou, no. 208 (1783).

Microfilm: 1657.

Morbihan

1894

262 L'ancien droit dans le Morbihan . . . par Emile Chénon. Vannes, Librairie Lafolye, 1894. 102 p.

Normandy

The first written compilation of Norman coutumes was the *Statuta et consuetudines Normannie,* which appeared in two parts, one written between 1199 and 1204,[69] and the other between 1218 and 1223.[70] Both parts were soon translated into French as the *Très-ancien Coutumier.* The second compilation of Norman law was the *Grand Coutumier,* a translation of the *Summa de legibus in curia laicali.*[71] The *Grand Coutumier* was more than just a compilation; it was an original work—methodical, scientific, and practical. It never achieved official status but had, throughout the duchy, the authority of a code.[72] The original two-part *Summa de legibus in curia laicali* was composed in the diocese of Coutances by a member of the Maucael family[73] between 1254 and 1258.[74]

There have always been close links between the laws of Normandy and those of England, and the anciennes coutumes of Normandy were closer to English than to French law. Norman law, as found in the coutumiers and coutumes, developed a strong regional character, which it retained even after union with the French crown.[75]

The official codification of the general coutume of Normandy was finally ordered by letters of March 22, 1577. After preparatory meetings in Rouen and elsewhere, publication took place in Rouen in 1583. The general coutume of Normandy was confirmed by an act of the Council on October 7, 1585, and by letters patent of October 14 the same year. The local coutumes of the duchy, a number of which limited the general coutume, were codified the following year. Finally, in 1600, under Henry IV, the titre des exécutions of the coutume of Normandy was reformed.[76]

ca. 1450–70 (manuscript)

263 [Grand coustumier de Normandie] ca. 1450–70. 242 l.

The Library of Congress *Coustumes de Normandie* is an unusual example of the *Grand Coutumier* because it is illustrated and decorated (parchment. 240 folios plus 2 paper guard leaves. 16.8 × 12.2 cm. 7 miniatures). Stylistic and codicological evidence suggest that the manuscript not only was designed for use in Normandy, but might well have been produced in that region during the third quarter of the fifteenth century.[77] The seven miniatures are reproduced in this volume; see also the note on illustrations, p. xi.

1483 (incunabulum)

264 Coutume du pays et duché de Normandie. Paris, Joannes de Prato, ca. 1483.

The *Grand Coutumier de Normandie*, text similar to no. 263.

1510

265 Le grãt coustumier du pays et duché de Normendie . . . selon la lecture de Jehan Andre . . . Caen, par Laurens Hostingue, pour Michel Angier et Jehan Mace, 1510. 174 l.

1513

266 Stilus supremae curie Parlamenti parisiensis atque tholosani . . . Sthephani Aufrerij . . . Rothomagi, 1513. 46, 6, 16, 11, 46 l.

Lettered on back of cover: Grand coustumier de Normandie. Rouen, 1515.

1515

267 Le grant coustumier du pays et duche de normendie tresutille et profitable a tous practiciens . . . Nouuellement Imprime, Rouen, Jehan Richard, 1515. 174, 32 l.

1523

268 Le grãd coustumier du pays et duche de Normendie . . . Rouen, Francoys Regnault, 1523. 209, 159 l.

1534

269 Le grand coutumier de Normandie avec la charte aux Normands, [par Guillaume le Rouille, d'Alençon] . . . Paris, Francoys Regnault, 1534. 146, 82 l.

1539

270 Le grand coustumier du pays & duche de Normendie/tresutile & profitable a tous practiciens . . . Composees par . . . maistre Guillaume le Rouille Dalencon . . . Nouuellemēt imprime a Rouen par Nicolas le roux pour Francoys regnault . . . 1539. 152, 82 l.

1552

271 Le covstvmier du pays, & duche de Normendie . . . Rouen, Martin le Mesgissier . . . 1552. 339 (i.e., 330) l.

1568

272 De consvetvdine Normaniae Gallica et Latina, diligenter visa, castigata, et commentariis . . . Liber I. Autore Tanigio Sorino Lessaeo . . . Cadomi, Apud Petrum Candelarium, 1568. 268 p.

Dedication signed: G. Lambert.

1574

273 Commentaires dv droict civil tant public que priué obserué au pays & duché de Normandie . . . Paris, Iaques du Puys, 1574. 728 p.

1578

274 Le covstvmier dv pays et dvché de Normendie . . . Auec plusieurs ordonnances . . . Roven, Martin le Mesgissier, 1578. 330 l.

1586

275 Covstvmes dv pais Normandie, anciens ressors, et enclaves d'icelvy. Paris, Pour Iacqves dv Pvys, 1586. 120 l.

On verso of leaf 120: Paris, Iean le Blanc . . . 1586.

Dedication signed: G. Lambert.

1587

276 Covstvmes dv pais de Normandie, anciens ressors, et enclaves d'icelvy. Paris, Iacqves dv Pvys, 1587. 120 l.

1589

277 Covstvmes dv pays de Normandie, anciens ressorts et enclaves d'icelvy. L'Isle, Gvillavme des Marescs, 1589. 168 p.

1594

278 Covstvmes dv pays de Normandie, anciens ressors & enclaues d'iceluy . . . Auec vne table tres-ample & narratifue de chasque article. Roven, Martin le Mesgissier, 1594. 119 l.

1596
279 Covstvmes dv pays de Normandie, anciens ressors, & enclaues d'iceluy. Caen, Iaques Mangeant, 1596. 182 l.

1614
280 La covstvme reformée dv pays et dvché de Normandie, anciens ressorts et enclaues d'iceluy. Avec les commentaires, annotations, et arrests . . . par Iosias Beravlt . . . 2. ed. Roven, D. dv Petit Val, 1614. 1064 p.

1626
281 Commentaires svr la covstvme reformée dv pays et dvché de Normandie, anciens ressorts & enclaues d'iceluy, . . . par Iacqves Godefroy. Roven, David du Petit Val, 1626. 2 v. in 1.

1632
282 La covstvme reformée dv pays et dvché de Normandie, anciens ressorts et enclaves d'icelvy. Avec les commentaires, annotations & arrests . . . par Iosias Beravlt . . . 4. et dernière éd. reueuë & augm. Roven, D. du Petit Val, 1632. 668 (i.e. 866) p.

1660
283 La covstvme reformée dv pays et dvché de Normandie, anciens ressorts et enclaves d'icelvy. Avec les commentaires, annotations & arrests . . . par Iosias Beravlt. 6. et derniere ed., rev. et avgm. Roven, la vefue de D. Dv Petit Val, 1660. 788, 153, 12 p.

1684
284 La coutume reformée du païs et duché de Normandie, anciens ressorts et enclaves d'iceluy. Commentée par Josias Berault, Jacques Godefroy, & d'Aviron . . . Rouen, D. Berthelin, 1684. 2 v.

1694–
285 La coutume reformée du païs et duché de Normandie. Commentée par Henry Basnage . . . 2. & nouv. ed., rev., cor. & augm. par l'auteur . . . Rouen, la veuve d'A. Maurry, 1694–

1696
286 Metode pour liquider les mariages avenans des filles dans la Coûtume generale de Normandie, & dans la Coûtume particuliere de Caux . . . Par Estienne Everard . . . Rouen, P. Ferrand & A. Maurry, 1696. 208 p.

1704
287 Coutume de Normandie, expliquée par Pesnelle. Avec les arrêts & réglemens de la cour . . . Rouen, Maurry, 1704. 576, 48 p.

1707
288 La coutume de Normandie reduite en maximes selon le sens litteral, & l'esprit de chaque article, par Pierre de Merville. Paris, H. Charpentier, 1707. 652, 47 p.

1709
289 Les oeuvres de Henri Basnage . . . contenant ses commentaires sur la Coutume de Normandie . . . 3. ed., rev., cor. & augm. par l'auteur . . . Rouen, Maurry, 1709. 2 v.

1720
290 L'esprit de la coutume de Normandie, avec un recueil d'arrets notables du même Parlement. Troisiéme et nouvelle edition . . . Rouen, Jean-Baptiste Besongne, le fils, 1720. 189, 168 p.

1727
291 Coutume de Normandie, expliquée par Pesnelle . . . 2. éd. Rouen, Jean-B. Besongne, le fils, 1727. 632, 112 p.

1731
292 Decisions sur chaque article de la Coutume de Normandie, et observations . . . Par Pierre de Merville . . . Rouen, C. Ferrand, 1731. 747 p.

1732
293 Decisions sur chaque article de la coutume de Normandie, et observations . . . Par Pierre de Merville. Paris, A. Mesnier, 1732. 747 p.

1742
294 Coutumes du pays et duché de Normandie, anciens ressorts & enclaves d'icelui, avgmentées . . . par les textes d'Aviron & de Berault . . . Nouv. & derniere ed. Rouen, J.-B. Besongne, 1742. 24, 659, 36 p.

1742
295 Principes généraux du droit civil et coutumier de la province de Normandie . . . Rédigées sur trois objets. Des personnes, des choses, & des actions . . . Par Charles Routier . . . Rouen, Pierre le Boucher, 1742. 632 p.

1754

296 Coutumes du pays et duché de Normandie, anciens ressorts & enclaves d'icelui, augmentées de plusieurs édits . . . rendus depuis 1666 jusqu'en 1753 . . . Nouv. éd. Rouen, Impr. de feu J. Besongne, 1754. 718 p.

1759

297 Coutume de Normandie, expliquée par Pesnelle . . . 3. éd. Avec les observations de Roupnel . . . Rouen, R. Lallemant, 1759. 732, 86 p.

1767

298 Texte de la coutume de Normandie, avec des notes sur chaque article . . . Par N***. Nouvelle edition . . . Paris, Durand Neveu, Rouen, la Veuve Besongne, 1767. 563 p.

1771

299 Coutume de Normandie, expliquée par Pesnelle . . . 4. éd., avec les observations de Roupnel de Chenilly . . . Rouen, R. Lallemant, 1771. 2 v.

1773

300 Coutume de Normandie. Avec l'ordonnance de 1667, & celle de 1670. Augm. d'une instruction sur la marche de la procédure civile & criminelle. Bayeux, Veuve Briard, 1773. 1 v. (various pagings)

1776

301 Commentaires sur la coutume de Normandie, par Bérault, Godefroy, & la paraphrase de d'Aviron. Nouv. éd., augm. . . . Rouen, De l'imprimerie privilégiée; Paris, Knapen, 1776. 2 v. in 1.

1778

302 Nouveau commentaire portatif de la coutume de Normandie, par Etienne Le Royer de la Tournerie. 2. éd. Rouen, Impr. privilégiée, 1778. 2 v.

1779

303 Coutume de Normandie, dans un ordre naturel, par Le Conte . . . Nouv. éd., cor. & augm. Rouen, De l'Imprimerie privilégiée; Paris, Le Boucher, 1779. 484 p.

1783

304 Texte de la coutume générale de Normandie, des placités, et du réglement des tuteles, mis en ordre par Ducastel . . . Rouen, L. Oursel, 1783. 32, 411 p.

1839

305 Etablissements et coutumes, assises et arrêts de l'échiquier de Normandie, au treizième siècle (1207 a 1245); d'après le manuscrit français f. 2 de la Bibliothèque de Sainte-Geneviève . . . Par A. J. Marnier . . . Paris, Techener, 1839. 222 p.

1856

306 Les ruines de la coutume de Normandie, ou Petit dictionnaire du droit normand restant en vigueur pour les droits acquis. Par V. Pannier . . . 2. éd., précédée d'une notice bibliographique . . . , par Ed. Frère. Rouen, A. Le Brument; Paris, A. Durand, 1856. 34, 116 p.

"Editions des auteurs cités": p. 2.

1881–

307 Coutumiers de Normandie; textes critiques publiés avec notes et éclaircissements, par Ernest-Joseph Tardif . . . Rouen, E. Cagniard, 1881–

"Liste des documents manuscrits cités dans les notes et dans l'appendice."

1886

308 Les coutumes de Normandie, réglementées par l'édit de 1751 . . . Par Léon de Vilade. 6. éd. Paris, Durand, Pedone-Lauriel, 1886. 299 p.

1889

309 Des droits de la fille; ou, Du mariage avenant dans la coutume de Normandie. Paris, L. Larose et Forcel, 1889. 108 p.

1935

310 La coutume de Normandie. Histoire externe [par] Robert Besnier. Paris, Librairie du Recueil Sirey, 1935. 296 p.

Microfilm: 1612, 1620, 1678–81, 1684, 1707, 1731, 1746, 1759, 1767, 1771, 1776.

Poitou

The important coutume of Poitou applied to a large territory made up of all of Poitou, with seats at Poitiers, Fontenay le Comte, Niort, Montmorillon, Civray, Saint Maixent, Melle, and the islands of Noirmoutiers, Dieu, Gouin, the small Marche of Poitou, the sénéchaussée of Basse Marche, and the city and sénéchaussée of Dorat.[78] Because of its geographical location, Poitou was under the influence of both the coutumes of the north and the Roman law of the south.[79]

Before the official codification in 1514, the province of Poitou already had the *Vieux Coustumier de Poictou,* which is traditionally believed to have been drawn up in 1417 during the siege of the city of Parthenage. A manuscript in the Bibliothèque nationale (ms. fr. 12042, folio 101v) gives credit for the compilation of these laws to Jehan de Lambertière, bailli of Gatine, Jehan de la Chaussée, Loyset Moysen, Robert Tutant, Pierre Poigne, and Jacques Boutin.[80] This private work was first printed in Poitiers in 1486 and was reprinted in 1500, 1503, and 1508.[81] In 1514, during the reign of Louis XII, the coutume of Poitou, like those of La Rochelle and Angoumois, was first officially codified and published by commissioners Baillet and Barme. Later, after the procès-verbaux were lost, a royal letter of August 19, 1556, ordered a new codification and publication of the coutume of Poitou. This publication, by de Thou, Faye, and Viole, occurred in 1559.[82]

1548

311 Petri Rat . . . in patrias Pictonum leges, quas vulgus consuetudines dicit glossamata . . . Pictavii, ex officina Marnefiorum Fratrum, sub Pelicano, 1548. 226 l.

1560

312 Covstvmes de novveav reformees du comté, & pais de Poictou, anciẽs ressorts & enclaues d'iceluy, mises & redigees par escript, . . . par Christofle de Thou . . . Barthelemy Faye, & Iacqves Viole . . . Paris, Sur le pont sainct Michel, 1560. 94, 24 l.

1584

313 Andrea Tiraqvelli . . . Ex commentariis in pictonvm consvetvdines Sectio de legibus connubialibus, & iure maritali . . . Lugdvni, Gvlielmvm Rovillivm, 1584. 512 p.

1586

314 Coustumes du pays & comté de Poictov, commentees . . . par Theveneav . . . annotations de Charles du Moulin . . . ensemble les resolutions tirees des escripts de Tiraqueau . . . Poictiers, Bouchetz freres, 1586. 425 p.

1609

315 Petri Rat . . . In Pictonum leges, quas vvlgvs consuetudines dicit, glossemata . . . Augustoriti Pictonum, Ex officina Antonii Mesnier, 1609. 630 p.

1625

316 Covstvmes dv comté et pays de Poictov, anciens ressorts et enclaues d'icelvy. Avec les annotations . . . par Iacqves Barravd . . . Poictiers, I. Thoreav, 1625. 489, 98 p.

1636

317 Observations svr la covstvme dv comté et pays de Poictov, anciens ressorts et enclaves d'icelvy . . . Par Iean Lelet. Poictiers, Ivlian Thoreav, 1636. 863 p.

1659

318 Responsa Io. Bosselli Borderii . . . et Ioan. Constantii . . . Ad varias qvaestiones ipsis svo cvivsqve tempore propositas, in consuetudinem Pictonum, ab anno 1530 . . . Avgvstoriti Pictonvm, sumptibus Ioannis Flevriav . . . et viduae Eliae Bravd, 1659. 634, 48 p.

1683

319 Observations sur la coustume du compté et pays de Poitou anciens ressorts . . . par Jean Lelet . . . Reveüe, corrigée & augmentée, par Jean Filleau. Poictiers, Robert Courtois, Michel Amassard, et Jean Babtiste Braud, 1683. 2 v. in 1.
   See also Senlis, no. 186 (1703).

1723

320 Observations sur la coutume de Poictou, par Jean Lelet . . . corrigées . . . par Jean Filleau. Poitiers, Louis Gillet, 1723. 888 p.

1727

321 Coûtumier general, ou Corps et compilation de tous les commentateurs sur la coûtume du comté et pays de Poitou, avec . . . les notes de Charles Du Moulin . . . Par Joseph Boucheul . . . Poitiers, J. Faulcon, 1727. 2 v.
   Printer's mark on title pages.

1762

322 Traité des fiefs sur la coutume de Poitou, par Jean-Baptiste-Louis Harcher. Augm . . . par M. ***. Poitiers, J. F. Faulcon, 1762. 2 v. in 1.

1764

323 Principes généraux de la coutume de Poitou,

ou les articles du texte . . . par Louis Marquet. Poitiers, J. Felix Faulcon, 1764. 497 p.

1956
324 Le vieux coustumier de Poictou [par] René
Filhol. Bourges, Editions Tardy, 1956. 328 p.

Microfilm: 1609, 1625, 1710, 1762.

Roville

See Normandy, no. 269 (1534).

Judicial duel, folio 89. When a plaintiff's accusations were denied by the defendant, the case often had to be settled by duel. At noon on the appointed day, four *chevalliers* took the two *champions* to a *champ*. After an elaborate, prescribed ritual of prayers and oaths, the opponents fought. "Se le deffêdeur poeut deffendre soÿ tant que les estoilles pairent au ciel Il aura vaĩcu la partie. . . ." In this miniature, evenly spaced, five-pointed gold stars stud the darkening sky. (folios 115r to 117r)

Coutumes of the Northern Region

The northern region of France includes Flanders, Artois, Picardy, and Vermandois. In the tenth century Flanders was divided into two parts—Walloon (French-speaking) and Flemish. Walloon Flanders owed allegiance to the king of France, while Flemish was considered a fief of the empire. The coutumes of French Flanders included those of Lille, Douai, Orchies, Grammont, Cambrai, Mortagne, Saint-Amand, Saint-Vinox, plus a large number of local coutumes.[83]

Abbeville

See coutume of Ponthieu.

Amiens

The first charter of Amiens was an agreement with Counts Guy and Yves in 1084. In 1117 the bishop, in an effort to gain the sympathies of the people, gave to Amiens a charter of commune. King Philip Augustus renewed and confirmed this charter in 1185 and 1190 and stipulated at the same time that the city of Amiens would always be linked to the crown of France. Another confirmation of the charter was given in 1209.[84]

The official local coutume of Amiens, an important coutume, was one of the earliest codified—in 1496. It covered a large territory—almost all of Artois, in addition to the Amiénois itself.[85] The general coutume of Amiens was codified in 1507,[86] but it seems to have met with resistance; many places claimed that they had their own local coutumes. A reformed coutume of Amiens was published in 1567 by commissioners de Thou, Faye, and Viole.[87] *See also* Beauvaisis, no. 64 (1615).

1653
325 Les covstvmes generales dv bailliage d'Amiens. Commentees par Adrian de Hev . . . Paris, Gervais Alliot, 1653. 741, 141 p.

1662
326 Commentaire svr la covstvme generale dv bailliage d'Amiens . . . Par Iean dv Fresne. Paris, Estienne Mavcroy, 1662. 478, 83 p.

1683
327 Coustumes tant generales que particulieres du bailliage d'Amiens. Avec les notes de Charles Du Molin et autres remarques particulieres de Jean-Marie Ricard. Amiens, Veuve de R. Hubault, 1683. 454 p.

1713
328 Traité des donations entre-vifs et testamentaires, ensemble la Coutume d'Amiens commentée. Dernière ed., augm. de nouvelles remarques. Paris, Guignard & C. Robustel, 1713. 2 v.

1734
329 Traité des donations entre-vifs et testamentaires, avec la Coutume d'Amiens commentée. Augmentée du Traité . . . Nouv. ed. Paris, E. David, 1734. 2 v.

1754
330 Traité des donations entre-vifs et testamentaires, avec la Coutume d'Amiens commentée. Le Traité de la revocation . . . par Me ***. Et les nouvelles additions par Michel du Chemin. Paris, Knapen, 1754. 2 v.

1781
331 Coutumes du bailliage d'Amiens, commentées par Ricard. Nouvelle edition, augmentée. Abbeville, Devérité, 1781. 292, 34 p.

1854

332 Rapport sur un ouvrage de Bouthors . . . Intitulé: Coutumes locales du bailliage d'Amiens, par Dupin. Orléans, Coignet-Darnault, 1854. 28 p.

Arras

See also Gorgue, no. 357 (n.d.); Artois, no. 334 (1679) and no. 335 (1679).

1746

333 Coutumes locales, tant anciennes que nouvelles de la loy, banlieuë et echevinage de la ville d'Arras; de la loy, banlieuë & echevinage de la cité d'Arras . . . Paris, P.-G. Simon, 1746. 411 p.

Artois

Artois was Flemish from 804 until 1180, when it passed to France in the dowry arrangement of Isabelle of Hainaut at the time of her marriage to Philip Augustus. In 1237, the province was set up as a county by Louis IX for his son Robert, the first count of Artois.

The *Ancien Coutumier d'Artois* contained coutumes in use in that province in the thirteenth century; the coutumier was certainly in effect before 1315.[88]

In 1509, the count of Artois began the codification of the general coutumes of the country, and the work was continued more actively after the partition of 1525. No region had more local coutumes. The last local coutume to be codified in Artois was that of the seigneurie of Richebourck Saint Vaast in 1669.[89] *See also* Amiens, no. 326 (1662).

1679

334 Coustumes generales du comté d'Artois, avec celles de l'eschevinage d'Arras, bailliages de S. Omer . . . Derniere edition. Arras, J. B. Du Til, 1679. 736 p.

1679

335 Coustumes generales du comté d'Artois. Avec celles de l'Eschevinage d'Arras, des bailliages de S. Omer . . . Derniere edition . . . [n. p.] 1679. 736, 12 p.

1704

336 Coutumes générales d'Artois, avec des notes: par Adrien Maillart . . . Paris, N. Gosselin, 1704. 1016 p.

1739

337 Coutumes générales d'Artois, avec des notes; par Adrien Maillart. 2. éd. rev. & augm. par l'auteur. Paris, Jean Rouy, 1739. 42, 32, 1031 p.

ca. 1775 (manuscript)

338 Oeuvres de Robert Ansart sur la coutume générale d'Artois, distribués par ordre alphabétique et divises en chapitres et nombres [ca. 1775] 579 p.

no date (manuscript)

339 Cornuel. Remarques et observations sur plusieurs articles de la coutume generale d'Artois. 363 p.

1869

340 Exposé de la législation coutumière de l'Artois . . . Edmond Lecesne. Arras, A. Courtin, 1869. 617 p.

1883

341 . . . Coutumier d'Artois, publié d'après les manuscrits 5248 et 5249, fonds français de la Bibliothèque nationale, par Ad. Tardif . . . Paris, A. Picard, 1883. 160 p.

Microfilm: 1582, 1739, 1756, 1763, 1771.

Bailleul

1632(?)

342 Les coutumes des ville et chastellenie de Bailleul. [n. p., 1632?] 95 (i.e. 92) p.

Bouillon

The coutume of Bouillon was codified in 1618 by order of Ferdinand, bishop of Liège and duke of Bouillon.[90]

1568

343 Ordonnances de Monsieur le duc de Bvillon pour le reiglement de la ivstice de ses terres et seigneuries souueraines de Buillon, Sedan . . . Avec les coutumes generales des dictes terres . . . Paris, Imprimees . . . par R. Estienne, 1568. 189 p.

Title on spine: Ordon[nances] de Sedan.

Cambrai

The archbishop-duke of Cambrai, Louis de Berlaymont, had the *Covtvmes generales de la ville et
duché de Cambray* codified and published in 1574
(*see* no. 344). When the county of Cambrésis—the
region around Cambrai bounded by Flanders,
Hainaut, Artois, and Picardy—was reunited with
France, its coutumes were respected. In case of default by the coutumes, Roman law was applied.[91]
See also Mons, no. 380 (1663).

1691
344 Covtvmes generales de la ville et duché de
Cambray, pays et conté du Cambresis. Avec
une explication . . . Par Pinault sr. des
Jaunaux . . . Douay, Mairesse, 1691. 523 p.
  See also Mons, no. 382 (1700).

1932–55
345 Le droit coutumier de Cambrai, par E. M.
Meijers et A. S. de Blécourt . . . Haarlem,
H. D. Tjeenk Willink, 1932–55. 2 v.

Châlons

The coutume of Châlons, in Champagne, applied
also to some scattered regions in Vitry and in
Barrois.[92] *See also* Vermandois, no. 397 (1557).

1571
346 Covstvmes de Chaalons, & ressort du siege
dudit lieu, en ce qui est du bailliage de Vermandois. Redigées par escrit . . . par Christofle de Thou, Barthelemy Faye & Iacques
Viole. Reims, I. de Foigny, 1571. 29 (i.e.
31) p.

1615
347 Les covstvmes de Chaalons, avec commentaire
et recherches curieuses sur icelles, par Lovys
Godet. Chaalons, Gergain Nobily, 1615.
257 p.

1615
348 Covstvmes de Chaalons, & ressort du siege
dudit lieu, en ce qui est du bailliage de Vermandois. Redigées par escrit . . . par Christofle de Thou, Barthelemy Faye, & Iacques
Viole. Reims, S. de Foigny, 1615. 33 l.

1676
349 Covstvmes de Chaalons, avec les commentaires de Loüis Billecart . . . Paris, Charles

de Sercy, 1676. 628 p.
  See also Vermandois, no. 401 (1728).

Microfilm: 1615.

Flanders

Walloon Flanders belonged to France in the
Middle Ages, and it was French in language,
customs, and institutions. The municipal organization of most of the cities of the Low Countries was
notable as it reflected the cities' status as privileged
territories which enjoyed their own coutumes and
justice distinct from that of the neighboring lords.
With such an organization, the general coutume
played a completely secondary role, applying only
in cases of default of the local coutumes which existed almost everywhere. Walloon Flanders' general coutume was that of *La Salle, gouvernance, bailliage, and châtellenie of Lille,* and was never officially
codified. Holy Roman Emperor Charles V sent an
order in 1531 for the codification of the coutumes
of the *Pays de par deçà.* As a result of this order the
coutume for the city of Lille, the general coutume
of Hainaut, the private coutumes of the jurisdiction of Mons, of Ypres, and of Malines, and several
local coutumes of Artois were codified. Among
other local coutumes of Walloon Flanders, the
most important were those of the échevinage of
the city of Tournai, of the bailliage of Tournai, of
the gouvernance of Douai, and of the cities of Orchies and Gorgues.[93]

1664
350 Vlaems recht, dat is Costvmen ande wetten
ghedecreteert by de graven ende gravinnen
van Vlaenderen; . . . door Lavrence vanden
Hane. Ghent, Maximiliaen Graet, 1664.
1114 p.

1670
351 Nic. Burgundi Ad consvetvdines Flandriae
aliarumque gentium tractatus controver-
siarum . . . Editio ultima . . . Arnhemiae,
Apud Joh. Fridericum Hagium, 1670. 317,
58 p.

1676
352 Vlaemisch recht dat is costumen ende wetten
ghedecreteert by de graven ende gravinnen
van Vlaenderen . . . door Lavrens van den
Hane. 4. drvck. Vermeerdert met noch an-
dere costumen . . . t'Antwerpen, Michiel
Knobbaert, 1676. 1116, 42, 52 p.

1719
353 Les coustumes et loix des villes et des chastellenies du comté de Flandre, traduites en françois, par Le Grand. Auxquelles les notes latines & flamendes de Laurens vanden Hane sont jointes . . . Cambray, N. J. Douilliez, 1719. 3 v.

no date
354 Annotations, consultations et avis sur le droit coutumier, émanés des avocats les plus distingués au Conseil en Flandre et au Grand conseil de Malines, aux XVIIe et XVIIIe siècles. [n. p., n. d.] 322 p.

1868–
355 Coutumes des pays et comté de Flandre. [Quartier de Gand] Bruxelles, F. Gobbaerts, 1868–
      Vols. 1, 3, 4, 9, 14.

1902
356 Le régime successoral dans les coutumes de Flandre à l'exception des règles spéciales aux biens nobles. Lille, Camille Robbe, 1902. 242 p.

Gorgue
See also coutume of Flanders.

no date
357 Les coustumes locales et particulieres de la ville et bourgeoisie de la Gorgue et de la Loy d'Arras [n. p., n. d.] 18 p.

Guînes

The coutume of Boulenois applied in the county of Guînes. It was compiled in 1495 but was never formally published. Letters patent of Henry II in August 1550 ordered a second codification, which was prepared by Nicholas Dupré and Jean Aymery. In 1567, the general coutume of the county of Guînes was compiled and presented to those commissioners who were in charge of the revision of the coutume of Amiens. Apparently it was never confirmed.[94]

1856
358 Le livre des usaiges et anciennes coustumes de la conté de Guysnes, avec une introduction et des notes, par Tailliar . . . et un aperçu his-torique sur le comté de Guînes, par Courtois. Saint-Omer, Chanvin fils, 1856. 225 p.

Hainaut

Baudouin VI (of Hainaut, IX of Flanders) gave to Hainaut a general charter in the year 1200. There may have been an earlier general charter, in 1171, but it has not been confirmed. The charter of Baudouin was based on Salic law to some extent, and it also contained some borrowings from Roman law. The second general charter, of 1410, was completed by Princess Jaqueline of Holland, Bavaria, and Hainaut (d. 1436) on March 1, 1418.[95] Next came a charter of Emperor Maximilian on April 8, 1483 (before his coronation) and his son, Philip I of Castille (d. 1506).[96] Emperor Charles V endorsed the coutume of Hainaut, March 15, 1534.[97] New coutumes, codified for Hainaut and also for Valenciennes in 1619, were completed in 1624. The coutume of Hainaut applied in the regions of Mauberge, Landrecies, Avesnes, Beaumont, Chimay, Condé, Saint-Amand, and Quesnoy.[98]

1553
359 Loix, chartres et coustumes du noble pais et côte de Haynault . . . Anuers, Jehan Loy, 1553. 201 p.
      See also Mons, no. 380 (1663).

1664
360 Recveil de plvsievrs placcarts fort vtiles av pays de Haynnav, dont les chartes dvdit pays renvoient a qvantité d'icevx . . . Mons, Simeon de la Roche, 1664. 246 p.

1666
361 Les chartes novvelles dv pays et comté de Haynnav: Augmentées par Fortivs. Mons, la Vefue Simeon de la Roche, 1666. 486 p.

1736
362 Les chartes nouvelles du pays et comté Hainau, augmentées par Fortius . . . Mons, Gaspard Migeot, 1736. 429 p.

1750
363 La jurisprudence du Haynaut françois, contenant les coutumes de la province et les ordonnances de nos rois dans leur ordre naturel . . . par Antoine-François-Joseph Dumées. Douay, J. F. Willerval, 1750. 448 p.

1771

364 Exposition de la lettre et de l'esprit des chartes générales du Haynaut . . . aux coûtumes particulieres . . . Par Philippe-Joseph Raparlier . . . Douay, Derbaix freres, 1771. 591 p.

1946–

365 Institutions médiévales. Introduction au Corpus des records de coutumes et des lois de chefs-lieux de l'ancien comté de Hainaut. Mons, Union des imprimeries, 1946– 2 v.

1946

366 Corpus des records de coutumes et des lois de chefs-lieux de l'ancien comté de Hainaut. Mons, Union des imprimeries, 1946. 317 p.

Microfilm: 1666, 1736, 1750.

Lille

The compiled anciennes coutumes of Lille, collected in the fourteenth century by a clerk of the court of Lille named Jean Roisin, are sometimes called the *livre de Roisin*. This coutume was remarkable in that the municipal regime was highly organized, and Germanic traditions remained strong.[99] The coutume of Lille was officially codified in response to orders issued by Emperor Charles V in 1531.[100] For more information, *see* coutume of Flanders.

1569

367 Coutumes & vsages generaulx & particuliers de la Salle, bailliage & chastellenie de Lille, confirmez & decretez par Sa Majesté . . . Douay, Loys de Vvinde, 1569. 80 l.

1626

368 Covtvmes et vsages de la ville, taille, banlieve et eschevinage de Lille . . . de Iean le Bovck . . . Dovay, Baltazar Bellere, 1626. 462 p.

17th century (manuscript)

369 Pratique de Lille [Binder's title]. First half of 17th cent. 2 v.

1665

370 Covstvmes et vseages de la ville, taille, banlieve et eschevinage de Lille, confirmez et approvvez par l'Imperialle Maiesté . . . Lille, Nicolas de Rache, 1665. 48 p.

1673

371 Covstvmes et usages generaux de la salle, bailliage, et chastellenie de Lille . . . Lille, Nicolas de Rache, 1673. 160 p.

1687

372 Coustumes et usages de la ville, taille, banlieue et eschevinage de Lille . . . Lille, Jean-Baptiste de Moitemont, 1687. 48, 14 p.

1723

373 Coustumes et usages generaux de la salle, bailliage, et chastellenie de Lille, confirmées et decretées par Sa Majesté catholique: avec les coustumes locales . . . Augmentées des coustumes locales de la viscomté de Haubourdin & Ammerin . . . Lille, J. B. Henry, 1723. 160 p.

1788–90

374 Commentaire sur les coutumes de la ville de Lille et de sa châtellenie et conférences de ces coutumes . . . par feu Patou. Lille, Dumortier, 1788–90. 3 v.

1842

375 Franchises, lois et coutumes de la ville de Lille. Ancien manuscrit à l'usage du siège échevinal de cette ville . . . [par] Roisin. Publié avec des notes et un glossaire par Brun-Lavainne. Lille, Vanackere; Paris, Colomb de Batines, 1842. 470 p.

1932

376 Le livre Roisin, coutumier lillois de la fin du XIIIe siècle. Publié avec une introd. et un glossaire [par] Raymond Monier. Préface de A. de Saint-Léger. Paris, Domat-Montchrestien, 1932. 175 p.

Contains a list of manuscrits of the coutumes of Lille.

Luxembourg

This province was ruled by the general coutume of Luxembourg confirmed in 1623 by Philip IV of Spain (1621–65). When part of the duchy was reunited with France, it kept all of its privileges and anciennes coutumes. In 1661, the general coutumes of the city of Thionville and other cities and places in French Luxembourg were codified anew.[101]

1677
377 Covtvmes generales de la ville de Thionville, et des autres villes & lieux du Luxembourg-françois . . . Mets, François Bouchard, 1677. 146 (i.e. 126) p.

1867–69
378 Coutumes des pays, duché de Luxembourg et comté de Chiny, par M.-N.-J. Leclercq . . . Bruxelles, F. Gobbaerts, 1867–69. 2 v.
    Vol. 2 by Ch. Laurent.

1887
379 Coutumes des Pays, duché de Luxembourg et comté de Chiny, par Ch. Laurent. Deuxième supplément. Bruxelles, Fr. Gobbaerts, 1887. 485 p.

Mons

The city of Mons received two great charters in the Middle Ages, one in 1410 and the other in 1484. Before the 1410 charter, Salic law applied in domestic relations. The charter of 1410 recognized the right of daughters to inherit personal property.[102]

The special coutume of Mons, along with the general coutume of Hainaut, was codified in response to an order given by Emperor Charles V in 1531[103] and was confirmed by him on March 15, 1534.[104] According to this coutume, whenever it was silent on any point, the coutume of a neighboring territory, and not Roman law, was to be applied.[105]

1663
380 Loix, chartes et covstvmes dv chef-liev de la ville de Mons et des villes et villages y resortissans, auec . . . diuerses autres chartes & coustumes . . . Cambray, . . . Tournay, . . . & du pays de Liege. Mons, S. de la Roche, 1663. 51, 486 p.

1695
381 Loix, chartes et coustumes du chef-lieu de la ville de Mons . . . Mons, Erneste de la Roche, 1695. 116, 52 p.

1700
382 Loix, chartes et coutumes du chef-lieu de la ville de Mons, et des villes et villages y resortissans . . . de . . . Cambray, . . . Tournay, . . . & du pays de Liege. Mons, Erneste de la Roche, 1700. 548 p.

1739
383 Les loix, chartes et coutumes anciennes du Souverain Chef-Lieu de la ville de Mons, . . . Mons, Michel Varret, 1739. 72, 60, 10, 12 p.

Peronne

The coutume of Peronne, like that of Amiens, was published in 1567 by commissioners de Thou, Faye, and Viole.[106]

1621
384 Covstvme dv govvernement de Peronne, Montdidier, & Roye. De novvel corrigé. Paris, Charles le Qvevx, 1621. 203 p.
    See also Amiens, no. 326 (1662).

Picardy

The ancien coutumier of Picardy was drawn up by an unknown author in the first quarter of the fourteenth century.[107] Picardy included at least five general coutumes, those of Peronne, Ponthieu, Amiens, Boulenois, and Calais.[108]

1726
385 Le coutumier de Picardie, contenant les commentaires de Heu, Dufresne, Ricard, Gosset, Le Caron, La Villette, Dubours, Le Roy de Lozembrune . . . Paris, Aux Dépens de la Société, 1726. 2 v.

1840
386 Ancien coutumier inédit de Picardie, contenant les coutumes notoires, arrêts et ordonnances des cours, assises, et autres juridictions de Picardie, au commencement du quatorzième siècle (1300 à 1323.) Publiés d'après le manuscrit français n. 9822–3 de la Bibliothèque royale, par A. J. Marnier . . . Paris, Téchener, 1840. 187 p.

Ponthieu

This coutume was contained in part 2 of the ancien coutumier of Picardy. It was a private compilation drawn up by a jurisconsult between 1300 and 1325.[109] The coutume of Ponthieu was officially codified in 1495, but it was not decreed until 1507, by Carmone and de Besançon.[110]

1662 (manuscript)

387 Project de réformation des coutumes tant générales de la sénéchaussés et comté de Ponthieu que locales et particuliers de la ville et banlieue d'Abbeville [n. p.] 1662.

See also Amiens, no. 326 (1662).

Reims

The territory of Reims was never placed under the immediate power of the counts of Champagne. It formed a special feudal county for the benefit of the archbishop.[111]

The coutume of Reims, codified in 1481, had an original character because it was formed under the influence of the échevinage of the city. It appears that this first draft of the coutume may not have removed all ambiguities in the law, because inquests by turbe to determine the meaning of certain obscure texts were still being held in the sixteenth century.[112] *See also* Vermandois, no. 397 (1557).

1615

388 Covstvmes de la cité & ville de Reims, villes & villages regis selon icelles . . . par Christofle de Thou, Barthelemy Faye, & Iacques Viole. Reims, S. de Foigny, 1615. 61 l.

1665

389 Covstvmes de la cite et ville de Rheims, villes et villages regis selon icelles . . . Par Iean Baptiste de Bvridan. Ovvrage posthvme donné au public par les soins de Bvridan son fils. Paris, L. Billaine, 1665. 854 p.

See also Vermandois, no. 401 (1728).

1840–52

390 Archives législatives de la ville de Reims; . . . par Pierre Varin. Paris, Crapelet, 1840–52. 4 v.

Microfilm: 1665.

Saint-Amand

1934

391 Des lois et coutumes de Saint-Amand, par E.-M. Meijers . . . et J.-J. Salverda de Grave . . . Haarlem, H. D. Tjeenk Willink, 1934. 268 p.

Also lists manuscripts. For the first and second parts, modern French translation is given

opposite the old French text; the third and fourth parts are not translated from the old French.

Saint-Bauzeil

The charter of June 30, 1281, contains privileges and coutumes conceded to the inhabitants of Saint-Bauzeil by William and Pierre of Saint-Sernin.[113]

1881

392 Coutumes de Saint-Bauzeil (Ariège). Texte inédit de 1281 publié avec préface et notes, par F. Pasquier. Paris, L. Larose et Forcel, 1881. 40 p.

Saint-Omer

The citizens of Saint-Omer took advantage of the accession of a new count, Guillaume Cliton, to declare themselves a commune. On April 14, 1127, the count conceded to them certain privileges and franchises which were later renewed several times.[114] *See also* Artois, no. 334 (1679) and no. 335 (1679).

1744

393 Coutumes particulieres et locales des bailliages, villes et banlieues de S. Omer et d'Aire, et des chatellenies d'Audruwicq Saint Omer, D. Fertel, 1744. 106, 30 p.

Sedan

The coutume of Sedan was officially established in writing in 1568, by order of Henri Robert de la Marck, duke of Bouillon and sovereign lord of Sedan.[115] *See also* Bouillon, no. 343 (1568).

1909

394 Etude sur le droit matrimonial dans la coutume de Sedan, par Ch. Cousin. Paris, Arthur Rousseau, 1909. 217 p.

Tournai

See also Mons, no. 380 (1663) and no. 382 (1700).

1778–

395 Les coutumes, stils et usages, le l'échévinage de la ville et cité de Tournay . . . Tournay, N. Jovenau, 1778– vol. 2 only.

1923

396 Coutumes de la ville de Tournai par L. Verriest . . . Bruxelles, J. Goemaere, 1923. vol. 1, 516 p.

Vermandois

The *Coutumes des pays de Vermendois et ceulx de envyron* were composed by a practicing lawyer of Saint-Quentin in 1448. This coutumier served for the codification in 1507 of the coutume, which was reformed in 1556.[116]

The coutume of Vermandois was very important. It covered all of that part of Vermandois which was later included in the Ile-de-France and Picardy. This country comprised four of the six ecclesiastical peerages—the archbishopric of Reims and the bishoprics of Laon, Châlons, and Noyon.[117] The coutume of Vermandois was drawn up in response to the same letters patent of August 19, 1556, and by the same commissioners as the coutumes of Etampes, Montfort-l'Amaury, Mantes, and Meulan—de Thou, Faye, and Bourdin.[118]

The creation of a general coutume did not meet with resistance in Vermandois as it did in Artois. On the contrary, the codification of the coutume of Vermandois brought about the abrogation of many special usages, notably those of Soissons, Vervins, Vailly. There remained in the district only four local coutumes, those of Noyon, Saint-Quentin, Ribemont, and Coucy. Other parts of Vermandois were ruled by two general coutumes, those of Châlons and of Reims, whose territories later became part of Champagne.[119]

1557

397 Covstvmes generales et particvlieres dv bailliage de Vermandois . . . de Laon, qve des prevostés et anciens ressorts d'icelvi, comme Rheims, Chaalons, Noyon, Saint Qventin, Ribemont, Covcy et autres. Mises & redigées par escrit . . . au mois de nouembre 1556. Rheims, N. Bacquenois, 1557. 277 p.

See also Châlons, no. 346 (1571) and no. 348 (1615).

1616

398 Covstvmes dv bailliage de Vermandois en la cité, ville, baillieue & preuosté foraine de Laon. Mises & redigees par escrit . . . par Christofle de Thou, Barthelemy Faye, & Iacques Viole au mois de novembre 1556. Reims, S. de Foigny, 1616. 108 l.

1630

399 Les covstvmes generales dv bailliage de Vermandois, en la cité, ville, banlieve, & preuosté foraine de Laon. Et les particulieres de Ribemont, Sainct Quentin, Noyon, & Coucy. Avec commentaires . . . par Iean Baptiste Bvridan. Reims, Nicolas Hecart, 1630. 1107, 54 p.

1688

400 Coûtumes generales et particvlieres du Bailliage de Vermandois. Conferées ensemble. Avec notes & observations. Par Claude de la Fons . . . Nouvelle edition. Metz, François Bouchard, 1688. 457 p.

1728

401 Le coutumier de Vermandois, contenant les commentaires de Buridan & de La Fons, sur les coutumes de Vermandois: de nouvelles observations sur les mêmes coutumes, par d'Hericourt . . . les commentaires de Godet & de Billecart, sur celle de Chalons: de Buridan, sur Rheims: de Vrevin, sur Chaulny . . . Paris, Au dépens de la Societé, 1728. 2 v.

1858

402 Coustumes des pays de Vermendois et ceulx de envyron, publiées d'après le manuscrit inédit des Archives du département de l'Aube, par C.-J. Beautemps-Beaupré . . . Paris, A. Durand, 1858. 191 p.

Meeting near town, folio 111. Two groups of men convene in a field outside the city walls to examine some land that is the subject of a lawsuit. The inspection of land or other immovable objects in dispute, with the many restrictions and conventions controlling the number and character of witnesses and the method of recording, is mentioned several times in the *Coustumes*. "Cest brief doit estre envoyé au sergent de lespee de la baillie et quant il aura receu il doit assigner iour a celluy qui se plaint de tenir la veue et y doit semondre lautre partie pour la veue soustenir et iusques a xx homes des plus prouchains de la terre et des mieulx creables q̃ ne soient souppeconeux a lune partie ne a lautre ne parent et se doivent estre tieulx que len croye que ils sachent la verite de la querelle et pardevant eulx doit estre la terre arrestee en la main au prince." (folio 146r)

Coutumes of the Eastern Region

The provinces of the eastern region of France were Champagne, Lorraine, Alsace, and the two Burgundies.

Alsace

The province of Alsace kept its own law and usages after its union with France. This ancient law was a coutumier, often carrying on very old usages. For the most important cities, there were also municipal statutes, some of which were revised in the sixteenth century. In addition, Roman law was especially developed in Alsace in the sixteenth century, as it was in Germany. The local statute or coutume was applied first; if this failed, the general coutume was used. Roman law was used only as a last resort. One of the most widespread local coutumes, that of the little city of Ferrette, was adopted in a large part of the Haute Alsace.[120] *See also* Ferrette, no. 447 (1870).

Bar-le-Duc

Until 1571, Bar-le-Duc was ruled by the 1506 coutume of Sens, upon which its official coutume was later modeled.[121] In 1571, as a result of an agreement between the king of France and the duke of Lorraine and Bar, commissioners were designated to codify the coutumes of Bar-le-Duc, Saint-Mihiel, Clermont-en-Argonne, and Bassigny. Those of Bar-le-Duc were officially codified October 14, 1579, and registered at the parlement of Paris, December 4, 1581.[122] For more information, *see* coutume of Sens.

1711
403 Nouveau commentaire sur la coutume de Bar-le-Duc, conferée avec celle de St. Mihiel dont le texte est joint . . . Par Jean Le Paige l'aîne . . . 2. ed. Bar-le-Duc, Jean Lochet [1711] 182 (i.e. 482), 31, 61 p.

Bassigny

In 1571, as a result of an agreement with the king of France, the duke of Lorraine and Bar designated commissioners who were responsible for the codification of the coutumes of Bar-le-Duc, Saint-Mihiel, Clermont-en-Argonne, and Bassigny. Those of Bassigny were completed in 1580.[123] For more information, *see* coutume of Sens.

1607
404 Covstvmes generales dv bailliage dv Bassigny . . . Av Pont-a-Movsson, Melchior Bernard, 1607. 118 l.

Bresse

1698
405 Explication des statuts, coutumes et usages observés dans la province de Bresse, Bugey, Valromay, et Gex . . . Par Philibert Collet. Lion, Claude Carteron, 1698. 2 v. in 1.

1729
406 L'usage des pays de Bresse, Bugey, Valromey et Gex, leurs statuts, stil et édits, divisé en deux parties. Par Charles Revel. Nouv. éd. Augmentée de plusieurs annotations . . . Bourg en Bresse, Joseph Ravoux, 1729. 2 v. in 1.

Burgundy

The general coutume of the duchy of Burgundy governed a very extensive territory which included five large bailliages—those of Auxois, Montagne or Châtillon-sur-Seine, Dijon, Autun, and Châlon-sur-Saône. The general coutume of the county of Burgundy covered all of Franche-Comté and the bailliages of Amont, Aval, Dôle, and Besançon. The Etats of the duchy and those of the county of Burgundy had asked for a codification of their coutumes. On March 11, 1457, Duke Philip the Good of Burgundy (1419–1467) sent letters ordering the codification of the coutume of the county. The coutume of the duchy was confirmed on August 26, 1459, and that of the county on December 28 of the same year.[124]

A reform of the coutume of the duchy, ordered and postponed several times, was confirmed by the parlement at Dijon, December 15, 1575.[125]

no date (manuscript)
407 Remarques et decisions de Iobelot, premier president au Parlement de Besançon, sur la Coutume du comté de Bourgogne. [n. d.] 632 p.

1517
408 Commētaria Bartholomei de Chasseneuz . . . in consuetudines ducatus Burgūdie principaliter, et totius fere Gallie consecutiue. Lugduni, Impressa in edibus Jacobi Marechal, sumptibus Symon Vincent, 1517. 382 l.

1528
409 Reportoriū: . . . in Cōmentaria . . . Bartholomei de Chasseneuz . . . super Cōsuetudinibus Burgūdie. Lugduni, Antony du Ry, 1528. 415 l.

1534 (i.e. 1535)
410 Le grant coustumier de Bourgogne. Bartholomei a Chasseneo . . . tertia recognitio commētariorum in consuetudines ducatus Burgundie . . . Parisiis, F. Regnavlt, 1534 [i.e. 1535] 312, 47 l.
    Provides a list of the editors of this coutume.

1552
411 Consvetvdines dvcatvs Bvrgundiae, feréqve totivs Galliae, commentariis D. Bartholomaei à Chassenaeo . . . Lvgduni, Apud Antonium Vincentium, 1552. 1528 p.

1565
412 Conference Generale de la covstvme dv dvche de Bovrgongne avec tovtes les avtres covstvmes de France . . . par I. Bovvot. [n. p.] 1565. 576, 96, 36 p.

1574
413 Barthol. à Chassenaeo . . . commentarii in consvetvdines dvcatvs Bvrgvndiae, feréqve totius Galliae . . . Lvgdvni, Apud Bartholomaeum Vincentium, 1574. 1528 col.

1582
414 Consvetvdines dvcatvs Bvrgvndiae . . . Bartholomaei a Chassenaeo. Lvgdvni, Apud Bartholomaeum Vincentium, 1582. 1528 p.

1585
415 Arnoldi Ferroni . . . In consvetvdines Bvrdigalensivm Commentariorum. Lvgdvni, Apvd Antonivm Gryphivm, 1585. 336 p.

1588
416 Sommaire explication des articles de la covstvme dv pays et dvche de Bourgongne . . . par Claude de Rubys. Reueu corr. & augm. par l'autheur. Lyon, Benoist Rigavd, 1588. 288 p.

1590
417 Consvetvdines Dvcatvs Bvrgvndiae, fereqve totivs Galliae: Commentariis D. Bartholomaei à Chassenaeo . . . Francofvrti, Martini Lechleri, 1590. 1437 col.

1604
418 In Consvetvdines generales comitatvs Bvrgvndiae observationes . . . Authore Henrico Bogveto Dolano . . . Lvgdvni, apud Ioannem Pillehotte, 1604. 420 p.
    Publisher's device on title page: Dedicatory epistle by Henricvs Bogvetvs dated: 1603.

1616
419 Consvetvdines dvcatvs Bvrgvndiae, fereqve totivs Galliae commentariis D. Bartholomaei à Chassenaeo . . . Vltima haec editio . . . Coloniae Allobrogvm, Sumptibus S. Crispini, 1616. 1798 col.
    See also Franche-Comté, no. 448 (1619–20) and no. 449 (1619).

1632
420 La covstvme de Bovrgongne . . . par I. Bovvot . . . Commentaire . . . par Hvgves Descovsv. Dijon, Pierre & Iaques Chouët, 1632. 586 p.

1635(?)
421 Epitome dv commentaire general svr la

covstvme de Bovrgongne . . . par Bovvot
. . . [n. p., 1635 ?] 251 p.

1636

422 Covstvmes generales dv pays et dvché de
Bovrgongne. Auec les Ordonnances particu-
lieres & anciens Reglemens de la Cour . . .
Diion, Clavde Gvyot, 1636. 396 p.

1642

423 Covstvmes generales dv pays et dvché de
Bovrgongne. Nouuellement reueuës, cor-
rigées & augmentées en sette derniere edition.
Diion, Antoine Grangier, 1642. 396 p.

1647

424 Consvetvdines dvcatvs Bvrgvndiae, feréqve
totivs Galliae: commentariis D. Bartholomaei
a Chassenaeo . . . Sumptibus Samuelis Crispini. Anno 1647. 1798 p.

1665

425 Covstvmes generales dv pays et dvché de
Bovrgongne, avec les annotations de
Begat . . . & du Depringles . . . Reue.,
corr., & augm. de plusieurs arrests, ausquelles
on a adjoûté les notes de Charles Dv Movlin.
Lyon, la vefve de P. Cvsset, 1665. 538 p.

1684

426 Consvetvdines dvcatvs Bvrgvndiae feréque
totivs Galliae Bartholomaei a Chassenaeo
commentariis amplissimis & doctissimis illus-
tratae. Hac postrema editione . . . Juliani
Mallety . . . Lvgdvni, Apud B. Vincentium,
1684. 1528 p.

1697

427 Instituts au droit coutumier du duché de
Bourgogne. Avec le texte de la coutume . . .
Dijon, Jean Ressayre, 1697. 279, 184 p.

1698

428 Coutume generale des pays et duché de
Bourgogne, avec le commentaire de Taisand . . . le commentaire de Chasseneuz, les
annotations de Begat . . . du sieur avocat
Despringles, & autres: a quoi on a joint les
notes de Charles du Moulin . . . Dijon, J.
Ressayre, 1698. 872 p.

1705

429 Instituts au droit coutumier du duché de
Bourgogne . . . Avec le texte de la Coûtume
. . . Dijon, Jean Ressayre, 1705. 391 p.

1717

430 La coutume du duché de Bourgogne, enrichie
des remarques de Philipes de Villers, Jean de
Pringles, & Jean Guillaume, avec le procés
verbal des conférences par Jean Begat. Dijon,
Antoine de Fay, 1717. 725 p.

1725

431 Commentaire sur le titre des successions de la
coutume du comté de Bourgogne. [n. p.]
1725. 262 p.
    Includes Traité des institutions contrac-
tuelles, 72 p.

1725

432 In Consuetudines generales comitatus Burgundiae observationes . . . Authore Henrico
Bogueto Dolano . . . Edito nova. Veson-
tione, Joan. Cl. Bogillot, 1725. 241 p.

1736

433 Coutume generale des pays et duché de
Bourgogne, avec les observations de François
Bretagne . . . Celles de Nicolas Perrier . . .
des notes de La Mare & Jehannin . . . Dijon,
A.J.-B. Augé, 1736. 635 p.

1742–46

434 Les coutumes du duché de Bourgogne. Avec
les anciennes coutumes . . . Et les observations de Bouhier . . . Dijon, A.J.-B. Augé,
1742–46. 2 v.
    Vol. 2 has imprint: A Dijon, P. de Saint.
    Contains a history of the commentaries of
this coutume.

1743

435 Commentaire sur le titre des successions de la
coutume du comté de Bourgogne, par
Dunod. [n. p.] 1743. 246 p.
    Traité des institutions contractuelles, 71 p.

1747

436 Coutume générale des pays et duché de
Bourgogne, avec le commentaire de Taisand . . . le commentaire de Chasseneuz, les
annotations de Begat, du sieur Avocat Despringles . . . A quoi on a joint les notes de
Charles du Moulin . . . Dijon, F. Desventes,
1747. 872 p.

1751–65

437 Traités sur diverses matiéres de droit françois
a l'usage du duché de Bourgogne & des autres
pays qui ressortissent au parlement de Dijon.

Par Gabriel Davot. Avec des notes de Jean Bannelier. Dijon, Veuve de J. Sirot, 1751–65. 8 v.

1787–88

438 Oeuvres de jurisprudence de Bouhier . . . Recueillies et mises en ordre . . . par Joly de Bevy. Dijon, Louis Nicolas Frantin, 1787–88. 2 v.

Includes the portrait of Bouhier.

1930

439 Le coutumier vaudois de Quisard et les coutumes du duché de Bourgogne. [Par Ernest Champeaux] Dijon, Bernigaud & Privat, 1930. 37 p.

Microfilm: 1574, 1582, 1647, 1684, 1788–89.

Champagne

All of the northern part of this province was subject to the coutume of the bailliage of Vitry en Perthois, called Vitry-le-Français. Another part of Champagne was ruled by the coutume of the bailliage of Chaumont-en-Bassigny and another part by the coutume of the bailliage of Troyes.[126] *See* coutumes of Vitry, Chaumont-en-Bassigny, and Troyes for more information. *Also see* Troyes, no. 475 (1600), no. 476 (1661), and no. 480 (1768); Chaumont-en-Bassigny, no. 445 (1733) and no. 446 (1733).

1956

440 L'ancien coutumier de Champagne (xiiie siècle). Ed. critique . . . par Paulette Portejoie . . . Poitiers, P. Oudin, 1956. 250 p.

Chaumont-en-Bassigny

Part of the province of Champagne was subject to the coutume of the bailliage of Chaumont-en-Bassigny. This coutume was codified by commissioners Baillet and Barme in 1494, but was not published until 1509.[127] *See also* general coutumes of France, no. 1 (1517).

1578

441 Les loix mvnicipales, et covstvmes generales dv balliage de Chaulmont en Bassigny . . . par Iean Gousset. A noble maistre Gabriel le Geneuois. Paris, Michel de Roigny, 1578. 79 l.

1579

442 Les loix mvnicipales, et covstvmes generales dv balliage de Chaulmont en Bassigny . . . par Iean Gousset. Paris, M. de Roigny, 1579. 79 p.

1623

443 Les loix mvnicipales, et covstvmes generalles dv balliage de Chaulmont en Bassigny . . . par Iean Gousset. A noble maistre Gabriel le Geneuois. Espinal, Pierre Hovion, 1623. 90 l.

See also Senlis, no. 186 (1703).

1722

444 Les loix muncipales et coûtumes generales du bailliage de Chaumont en Bassigny . . . par feu Jean Gousset. Chaumont, Gabriel Briden, 1722. 364 p.

See also Sens, no. 472 (1731).

1733

445 Coutume de Chaumont en Bassigny, nouvellement commentee & conferée avec les autres coutumes de Champagne. L'ancienne redaction de la même coutume faite en l'année 1494, qui n'a point encore paruë. Le texte de la coutume de Paris . . . par Juste de Laistre. Paris, Denys Mouchet, 1733. 484, 50, 122 p.

1733

446 Coutume de Chaumont en Bassigny, nouvellement commentee & conferée avec les autres coutumes de Champagne. L'ancienne redaction de la même coutume faite en l'année 1494, qui n'a point encore paruë. Le texte de la coutume de Paris . . . par Juste de Laistre. Paris, Gregoire-Antoine Du Puis, 1733. 484, 50, 122 p.

Ferrette

The coutume of the little city of Ferrette, one of the most widely used local coutumes, was adopted by a large part of the Haute Alsace, and, in 1707, by the city of Neubrisach.[128] For more information, *see* coutume of Alsace.

1870

447 Coutumes de la Haute-Alsace dites de Ferrette; pub. . . . par Ed. Bonvalot . . . Colmar, Barth et Held-Baltzinger; Paris, Durand et Pedone-Lauriel, 1870. 296 p.

The German text and the French translation are presented in parallel columns.

Franche-Comté

Franche-Comté, once a part of Burgundy, did not possess its own coutumier before the official codification of its coutume in 1459.[129] *See* coutume of Burgundy.

1619-20
448 Les covstvmes génerales de la Franche-Conte de Bovrgongne . . . Dole, A. Dominique, 1619-20. 390 (i.e. 384) p.

1619
449 Recveil des ordonnances et edictz de la Franche-conté de Bovrgongne par Messire Iean Pétremand. Dole, A. Dominique, 1619. 390 (i.e. 384) p.

Lorraine

This coutume was codified in 1594 under the auspices of Charles III, duke of Lorraine.[130] The coutume of Lorraine included three general coutumes, those of the bailliages of Nancy, Vosges, and Allemagne.[131]

1614
450 Covstvmes generales dv dvché de Lorraine es bailliages, de Nancy, Vosges et Allemagne. Nancy, Iacob Garnich, 1614. 61 l.

1634
451 Commentaire svr les Covstvmes de Lorraine . . . Par Pierre Canon . . . Espinal, Ambroise, 1634. 494 p.

1657
452 Les remarques de Abraham Fabert svr les coustumes génerales du duché de Lorraine, és bailliages de Nancy, Vosges et Allemagne. Metz, C. Bouchard, 1657. 539 p.

1682(?)
453 Coustumes generales anciennes et nouvelles du duché de Lorraine pour les bailliages de Nancy, Vosge, & Allemagne. [n.p.] Charles de Sercy [n.d.] 218 p.

1710
454 Coûtumes generales anciennes et nouvelles du duché de Lorraine pour les bailliages de Nancy, Vosges & Allemagne . . . Nancy, Paul Barbier, 1710. 193 p.

1725
455 Dissertation sur le titre X. des coutumes generales, anciennes et nouvelles du duché de Lorraine . . . Nancy, J. B. Cusson, 1725. 360 p.

1770
456 Coutumes générales du duché de Lorraine pour les bailliages de Nancy, Vosges & Allemagne. Nouv. éd. imprimée sur celle de Jacob Garnich de l'an 1614 et augm. . . . Nancy, Babin, 1770. 170 p.

1878
457 Les plus principalles et générales coustumes du duchié de Lorraine. Texte inédit précédé d'une introduction, par Ed. Bonvalot . . . Paris, Durand et Pedone-Lauriel, 1878. 133 p.

1887
458 Contribution à l'étude du droit coutumier lorrain; des différentes formes de la propriété: fiefs, censives, servitudes réelles, par Victor Riston. Paris, Librarie nouvelle de droit et de jurisprudence, 1887. 347 p.

Lorraine and Bar
See coutume of Lorraine.

Metz

Charles IX granted letters in 1569 for the codification of the coutumes of the city and countryside of Metz, but to no effect. In 1578, Henry III gave new letters, again without result. The Etats of Metz renewed their pleas in 1602, and Henry IV ordered the compilation of the coutume of Metz. Work began slowly, and the Etats were not convened for the publication of the coutume until 1611, in response to letters from Louis XIII. The coutume was printed in Metz in 1613. There were two kinds of coutumes of Metz, those for the city of Metz and surrounding countryside, and those for the bailliage and bishopric of Metz.[132]

1613
459 Covstvmes generales de la ville de Metz, & pays Messin . . . Metz, R. Fabert le Jeune, 1613. 111 p.

1683

460 Coutumes de l'eveché de Metz, avec les municipales de Ramberviller . . . Metz, François
Bouchard, 1683. 146 p.

1688

461 Coûtumes generales de la ville de Metz, et
pays messin. Corr. ensuite des résolutions de
trois Etats de ladite ville és années 1616, 1617
& 1618 . . . 2. ed. Metz, F. Bouchard, 1688.
168 p.

1698

462 Traité de la difference des biens meubles, et
immeubles de fonds et de gagieres, dans la
coûtume de Metz . . . Metz, Brice Antoine,
1698. 274 p.

1730

463 Coutumes générales de la ville de Metz et pays
messin, corrigées ensuite des résolutions des
trois-etats de ladite ville, és années 1616,
1617, & 1618 . . . Enrichies d'un commentaire . . . Premiere edition. Metz, Brice
Antoine, 1730. 406 p.
     Edited by Dilange. *Cf.* Barbier; also
Querard and Jöcher, not in this bibliography.

1732

464 Coutumes generales de la ville de Metz et pays
Messin, corrigées ensuite des résolutions des
Trois-Etats de lad. Ville, és années 1616, 1617,
& 1618 . . . Enrichies d'une commentaire . . . 2. ed. Metz, De l'Impr. de la Veuve
de Brice Antoine, 1732. 648 p.

1769

465 Coutumes générales de la ville de Metz et
pays-Messin . . . Nouvelle édition conforme
à celle imprimée en 1732. Metz, Joseph Collignon, 1769. 528 p.

1796

466 Recueil des loix, coutumes et usages observés
par les Juifs de Metz, en ce concerne leurs
contrats de mariage . . . Auquel on a joint
l'extrait qui en a été fait par feu Monsieur.
Lançon . . . Metz, la Veuve Antoine & fils,
1796. 271, 104 p.

1951–67

467 Le droit coutumier de la ville de Metz au
Moyen Age, publié par J. J. Salverda de
Grave, E. M. Meijers et J. Schneider.
Haarlem, H. D. Tjeenk Willink, 1951–67. 3 v.

val d'Orbey

This coutume was codified on the initiative of
Ribeaupierre. Maximin II began the work in 1513,
Guillaume II continued it in 1536, and Egenolphe
III finished it in 1564. The first two compilations
were in German, that of Egenolphe III in French.
Though not codified until the sixteenth century,
the coutume of val d'Orbey established very old
usages.[133]

1864

468 Les coutumes du val d'Orbey. Publiées avec
introd. et notes par Ed. Bonvalot. Paris, A.
Durand, 1864. 56 p.

Saint-Mihiel

In 1571, as a result of an agreement with
Charles IX of France, the duke of Lorraine and
Bar named the commissioners who were to be
responsible for codification of the coutume of Bar-
le-Duc, Saint-Mihiel, Clermont-en-Argonne, and
Bassigny. The coutume of Saint-Mihiel was completed in 1598. Additions were made in 1607 and
endorsed by Duke Henry two years later.[134]

1698

469 Coutumes du bailliage de Saint Mihiel . . .
Metz, Brice Antoine, 1698. 260 p.

1706

470 Coutumes du bailliage de Saint Mihiel . . .
Metz, Jean Antoine, 1706. 253 p.
     See also Bar-le-Duc, no. 403 (1711).

Sens

The territory of the general coutume of the bailliage of Sens lay between the bailliages of Troyes,
Chaumont, Montargis, Auxerre, and the two
Burgundies. The cities of Sens and Langres and
the county of Montsaujon were governed by local
coutumes. Some parts of Barrois were included in
the jurisdiction of the bailliage of Sens. The coutume of the region Sens was codified very early, in
1495, and published by commissioners Baillet and
de Besançon in 1506.
     The duke of Lorraine and Bar was summoned
in 1555 to take part in the codification of the coutume of the bailliage of Sens. Because he refused
to participate, it was decided that, contrary to his
wish, the duke's lands would be ruled in part by

the coutume of Sens. This situation continued until 1571, when an agreement was reached between the king of France, Charles IX, and Charles III, duke of Lorraine and Bar. It was decided that Barrois and that part of Bassigny which belonged to the duke would be districts of the bailliage of Sens, while appeals would continue to go to the parlement of Paris. The same treaty gave the duke of Lorraine the right to make ordinances and to codify coutumes. In the same year, 1571, Duke Charles named commissioners to direct the codification of the coutumes of the bailliages of Bar-le-Duc, Saint-Mihiel, Clermont-en-Argonne, and Bassigny. That of Clermont was codified in 1571, Bar in 1579, Bassigny in 1580, and Saint-Mihiel in 1598.[135]

1556

471 Covstvmes du bailliage de Sens & anciës ressorts d'iceluy, redigées . . . au mois de nouembre, l'an mil cinq cents cinquante cinq, par ordonance du roy. Sens, Gilles Richeboys, 1556. 95, 70, 174 p.

1731

472 Coutume des baillages de Sens et de Langres, commentée et conferée avec les coûtumes voisines, & specialement avec celle de Chaumont en Bassigny, par Juste de Laistre. Paris, les frères Osmont, 1731. 560 p.

1732

473 Coustumes du bailliage de Sens, et anciens ressorts d'iceluy, avec les notes de Jean Penon . . . Sens, André Jannot, 1732. 280 p.

1787

474 Conférence de la coutume de Sens . . . par Pelée de Chenouteau. Suivi de Détails historique sur le bailliage de Sens, rédigés par T.D.S. avocat en Parlement. Sens, Veuve Tarbé, 1787. 621 p.

Troyes

Part of the province of Champagne was ruled by the coutume of the bailliage of Troyes. The territories making up the bailliage of Troyes, the county of Joigny, and the châtellenie of Ile sur Serain were cut in two by the coutume of Sens and, in part, included in the coutumes of Sens, Auxerre, and Montargis. These coutume borders were strongly contested.[136] The coutume of Troyes was officially codified in 1494 and 1496 and published by Baillet and Barme in 1509.[137]

1600

475 Les covstvmes dv Bailliage de Troyes en Champaigne. Avec qvelqves annotations svr icelles. Par Pierre Ptihov. Paris, Abel l'Angelier, 1600. 222 p.

1661

476 Les covstvmes generales dv Bailliage de Troyes in Champagne. Avec les commentaites de Lovys Le Grand . . . Paris, chez la veufue Gervais Alliot, 1661. 716 p.

1681

477 Coustume du bailliage de Troyes, avec les commentaires de Louis Le Grand . . . Nouv. ed., rev., cor. & augm. par l'autheur. Paris, J. Guignard, 1681. 396, 384 p.

1715

478 Coutume du bailliage de Troyes, avec les commentaires de Louis Le Grand . . . 3. éd. augm. . . . Paris, Montalant, 1715. 396, 384 p.

1737

479 Coutume du bailliage de Troyes, avec les commentaires de Louis Le Grand . . . 4. éd. Paris, Montalant, 1737. 396, 384 p.

1768

480 Coutumes générales du bailliage de Troyes en Champagne . . . Par Marcilly. Paris, Hérissant fils, 1768. 645 p.
See also Lorris, no. 106 (1771).

Vaudémont

The decisive period for the coutume of Vaudémont came during the reign of Charles III, duke of Lorraine (1545-1608). The codification of the coutume was ordered September 5, 1602. After many false starts and an intervening war, Charles IV of Lorraine issued an ambiguous statement on October 17, 1661, forbidding his officials to alter the coutumes.[138]

1970

481 La coutume de Vaudémont. Nancy, Centre lorrain d'histoire du droit, 1970. 303 p.
Edited by Jean Coudert. List of manuscripts included.

1972

482 Le style de Vaudémont. Nancy, Centre lorrain d'histoire du droit, 1972. 173 p.

Verdun

The coutumes of Toul and Verdun were confirmed very late, in 1746, although the anciennes coutumes of Verdun had already been compiled privately.[139]

1678
483 Covtvmes generales de la ville et cité, evéché et comté de Verdvn, appellées communément les coûtumes & droits de Sainte Croix. Mets, Francois Bouchard, 1678. 114 p.

ca. 1750
484 Coutumes generales de la ville de Verdun et pays verdunois rédigées & réformées . . . Metz, François Antoine [1747?] 164 p.

1940
485 Le livre des droits de Verdun, publié par E.-M. Meijers . . . et J.-J. Salverda de Grave . . . Haarlem, H. D. T. Willink & zoon, 1940. 191 p.

Vitry-en-Perthois

The northern part of the province of Champagne was governed by the coutume of the bailliage of Vitry-en-Perthois, called Vitry-le-Français. The coutume of Vitry was published, in response to royal letters of September 18, 1509, by commissioners Baillet and Barme.[140] *See also* general coutumes of France, no. 1 (1517).

1618
486 Les covstvmes du bailliage de Vitry en Pertois.

Redigees . . . Revueuës & corr. par Charles du Molin . . . Reims, Simon & Iean de Foigny, 1618. 40 l.

1627
487 Les covstvmes du bailliage de Vitry en Pertois. Redigées . . . en l'An mil cinq cens & neuf. Recuuës & corrigées par Charles du Molin . . . Reims, Nicolas Constant, 1627. 80 p.

1660
488 Commentaire svr la Covstvme de Vitry. Par Charles de Salligny . . . Vitry, Qventin Senevze, 1660. 761 p.

1676
489 Coutumes de Vitry le François, avec le commentaire de Charles de Salligny . . . 4. ed. . . . Chaalons, J. Seneuze, 1676. 373 p.

1722
490 Coutumes du bailliage de Vitry en Perthois avec un commentaire; . . . Par Estienne Durand . . . Chaalons, C. Bouchard, 1722. 626 p.

1745
491 Dissertation qui prouve que le francaleu ne peut être sans titre dans la coutume de Vitry. Paris, Mesnier, 1745. 136 p.

1747
492 Re'futation de l'écrit intitulé Dissertation qui prouve que le francaleu ne peut être sans titre dans la coutume de Vitry. Vitry, Seneuze, 1747. 94 p.

Notes

1. Ernest D. Glasson, *Histoire du droit et des institutions de la France,* 8 vols. (Paris: F. Pichon, 1891), 8: 41.
2. Ibid., p. 65.
3. Ibid., 4:145.
4. See no. 55 of this bibliography, p. 1.
5. Glasson, 8: 59.
6. Edme Billon, *Coûtume du Comté et Bailliage d'Auxerre* (Paris: Jean Guigrart, 1693), p. 3.
7. Glasson, 8: 59.
8. Billon, p. 3.
9. Glasson, 8: 59.
10. Ibid., 4: 148–50.
11. Am. Salmon, *Coutumes de Beauvaisis,* vol. 1 (Paris: A. et J. Picard, 1970), p. xiv–xvi.
12. Georges Testaud, *La Coutume du comté de Clermont-en-Beauvaisis de 1496* (Paris: Librairie de la Société du Recueil Gal des lois et des arrêts, 1903), p.1.
13. Glasson, 8: 61.

14. Ibid.
15. Emile Chénon thinks that the coutume was not codified again until Charles VII's ordinance at Montils-les-Tours of April 1454, *Le "pays" de Berry et le "détroit de sa coutume"* (Paris: Société du Recueil Sirey, 1916), p. 97.
16. E. Mallet, *Thaumas de la Thaumassière, commentateur des coutumes de Berry* (Paris: E. Duchemin, 1915), pp. 5–15.
17. Chénon, p. 97.
18. Glasson, 8: 62.
19. Ibid., 4: 144.
20. Ibid., 8: 62.
21. Ibid., p. 57
22. Matthieu Auroux des Pommiers, *Coutumes générales et locales du pays et duché de Bourbonnais* (Riom: Dégoutte, 1780), pp. 1–11.
23. Henri Klimrath, *Etudes sur les coutumes* (Paris: Levrault, 1837), pp. 9–13.
24. Ibid., pp. 5–6.

25. Glasson, 8: 56.

26. Ibid., p. 50.

27. Ibid., p. 52.

28. Ibid., 4: 140.

29. Ibid., 8: 52.

30. Ibid., 4: 141.

31. Adolphe Tardif, *Coutumes de Lorris* (Paris: Alphonse Picard, 1885), pp. vi-viii.

32. Glasson, 8: 52.

33. Ibid., 4: 168.

34. Ibid., 8: 50.

35. Ibid., p. 66.

36. Ibid., p. 52.

37. Ibid.

38. Ibid., p. 50.

39. Klimrath, p. 7.

40. Glasson, 8: 59-60.

41. Ibid., 4: 131-35.

42. A. Tardif, *Coutumes de Lorris*, pp. vii-viii.

43. Glasson, 8: 54.

44. Ibid., 4: 152-59.

45. Ibid., 8: 41-44.

46. Ibid., p. 57.

47. Klimrath, p. 7.

48. Glasson, 4: 167.

49. Ibid., 8: 51.

50. Ibid., 4: 143-44.

51. Klimrath, p. 12.

52. Glasson, 8: 58.

53. Ibid., p. 67.

54. Ibid., 4: 110.

55. Klimrath, p. 13.

56. Glasson, 4: 110.

57. Ibid., 8: 76, 78.

58. Ibid., 4:111-19.

59. Marcel Planiol, *La Très Ancienne Coutume de Bretagne* (Rennes: J. Plihorn et L. Hervé, 1896), pp. 6-13.

60. Glasson, 8: 71.

61. Ibid., p. 80.

62. Klimrath, p. 13.

63. Glasson, 4: 105.

64. Ibid., 8: 80.

65. Klimrath, p. 14.

66. Glasson, 8: 78.

67. Ibid., 4: 110.

68. Ibid., 8: 78.

69. Ernest-Joseph Tardif, *Coutumiers de Normandie*, vol. 1 (Rouen: Esperance Cagniard, 1881), p. lxix.

70. Robert Besnier, *La Coutume de Normandie; histoire externe* (Paris: Librairie du Recueil Sirey, 1935), p. 53.

71. E.-J. Tardif, *Coutumiers de Normandie*, p. lxix.

72. Glasson, 4: 126.

73. Ernest-Joseph Tardif, *Les Auteurs présumés du Grand coutumier de Normandie* (Paris: L. Larose et Forcel, 1885), p. 49.

74. E.-J. Tardif, *Coutumiers de Normandie*, vol. 2 (Rouen: A. Lestrinant; Paris: A. Picard et fils, 1896), p. cxciv.

75. Glasson, 4: 124.

76. Ibid., 8: 67, 68, 70.

77. J. M. Caswell, "A Manuscript of *Coustume de Normendie* in the Library of Congress," prepared for a seminar in medieval manuscript illumination at the University of Maryland, College Park, 1974, under the direction of Prof. James D. Farquhar.

78. Glasson, 8: 78.

79. Ibid., 4: 107, 108.

80. René Filhol, *Le Vieux Coustumier de Poictou* (Bourges: Editions Tardy, 1956), p. 3.

81. Glasson, 4: 107.

82. Ibid., 8: 79.

83. Ibid., 4: 25.

84. Ibid., pp. 33-34. For clarification on Philip Augustus, see *La Grande Encyclopédie*, vol. 2 (Paris: H. Lamirault, 1886), p. 751.

85. Glasson, 8: 81.

86. Klimrath, p. 11.

87. Glasson, 8: 81.

88. Ibid., 4: 29-30.

89. Ibid., 8: 84.

90. Ibid., p. 92.

91. Ibid., p. 91.

92. Ibid., p. 86.

93. Ibid., pp. 87, 88.

94. Ibid., p. 83.

95. Ibid., 4: 27-28.

96. Klimrath, p. 7.

97. Glasson, 4: 27-28.

98. Ibid., 8: 90.

99. Ibid., 4: 25.

100. Ibid., 8: 90.

101. Ibid., p. 91.

102. Ibid., 4: 28.

103. Ibid., 8: 87, 88.

104. Ibid., 4: 28.

105. Ibid., 8: 91.

106. Ibid., p. 81.

107. Ibid., 4: 33.

108. Ibid., 8: 81.

109. Ibid., 4: 33.

110. Klimrath, p. 12.

111. Glasson, 4: 43.

112. Ibid., 8: 86.

113. F. Pasquier, *Coutumes de Saint-Bauzeil* (Paris: L. Larose et Forcel, 1881).

114. Glasson, 4: 32.

115. Ibid., 8: 92.

116. Glasson, 4: 36-37. In vol. 4 Glasson places the coutume of Vermandois in the northern region; in vol. 8 he places the coutume in the region of the center of France.

117. Ibid., 8: 85, 86.

118. Ibid., p. 50.

119. Ibid., pp. 85, 86.

120. Ibid., 8: 97-98.

121. Jean Le Paige, *Nouveau Commentaire sur la coutume de Bar-le-Duc* (Bar-le-Duc: J. Lochet, 1711), p. 5.

122. Glasson, 8: 94.

123. Ibid., p. 94.

124. Ibid., p. 99.

125. Klimrath, p. 21.

126. Glasson, 8: 92.

127. Ibid.

128. Ibid., p. 98.

129. Ibid., 4: 56.

130. Ibid., p. 47.

131. Ibid., 8: 97.

132. Ibid., p. 95.

133. Ibid., 4: 51-52.

134. Ibid., 8: 96.

135. Ibid., p. 93.

136. Ibid., pp. 92, 93.

137. Klimrath, pp. 7, 12.

138. *La Coutume de Vaudémont* (Nancy: Centre lorrain d' histoire du droit, 1970), pp. 8-13.

139. Glasson, 8: 96.

140. Ibid., p. 92.

A king of France giving a document to an archbishop, folio 227. This miniature is probably a symbolic representation of the kings of France giving coutumiers or chartes to the archbishops of Normandy. These agreements were renewed many times, as when the *Charte aux Normands* was reconfirmed by Philippe de Valois in 1339, by Charles VI in 1380, and by Louis XI in 1461.

Coutumes of Written Law Regions
(Pays de droit écrit)

The southern regions of France were droit écrit, rather than coutume, countries. These droit écrit areas are mentioned in a study of coutumes because many general and local coutumes and charters established privileges and often derogated droit écrit. In all of these territories of the Midi, customary law took second place to Roman law, but it was still important.[1]

All local coutumes in the Midi resemble each other, just as in the north collections of laws called *coutumes mères* served as models for other cities. The charters and coutumes of the Midi were more concerned with public law, administration, and justice than with private law.[2]

Agen

In the city of Agen, consuls were in charge of administration and aldermen rendered civil justice. However, these officials shared jurisdiction over justice with the count and, after the union of the city with the crown, with the king. The deliberations of the consuls and the aldermen since the year 1344 have been conserved in the archives of the city of Agen. It is possible that the codification of the ancienne coutume of the Agenais region took place in 1287 when the parlement of Paris ordered an inquest by turbe on an important point in a coutume of Agen.

Because of the domination of the English in the Agenais, a number of the communes there obtained true charters.[3]

1666
493 Reflexions singvlieres svr l'ancienne covstvme de la ville d'Agen . . . Par Jacques Dvcros. Agen, Jean Gayav, 1666. 642, 62, 40, 40 p.
See also Castel-Amouroux, no. 510 (1888).

1890
494 Les coutumes de l'Agenais, Mocliar-Monflan-quin, Saint-Maurin, par H.-Emile Rébouis. Paris, L. Larose et Forcel, 1890. 47 p.
Cataloged in the Law Library under coutume of Agenais.

1890
495 Les coutumes de l'Agenais, Nomdieu-Sauvagnas, par H.-Emile Rébouis. Paris, L. Larose et Forcel, 1890. 36 p.
Cataloged in the Law Library under coutume of Agenais.

Andorre

The inhabitants of Andorre remained faithful to the old usages longer than the people of other regions.[4] Indeed, the coutume of Andorre was never officially codified.[5]

1937
496 La coutume privée d'Andorre envisagée dans ses sources et dans ses institutions les plus originales . . . par Pierre Barbier . . . Paris, A. Rousseau, 1937. 157 p.

1938
497 La coutume privée d'Andorre envisagée dans ses sources et dans ses institutions les plus originales, par Pierre Barbier . . . Paris, A. Rousseau, 1938. 157 p.

Béarn

The anciens fors, or tribunals, of Béarn created a very complete collection of laws and usages, including public law, feudal law, civil law, procedure, and criminal law. They were compiled between the eleventh and thirteenth centuries and comprised four principal acts: the charter of Oloron (1080), the for of Morlâas (1101), the for of Trois Vallées

(1221), and the general for, of which the original date is unknown, but which was renewed in 1228.[6]

The coutume of Béarn was codified in 1551 and was authorized the same year by Henry II, the Valois king of Navarre and lord of Béarn.[7]

1552
498 Lòs fors, et costumas de Bearn. Imprimidas à Pauper Johan de Vingles et Henry Poyure, 1552. 180 p.

1682
499 Los fors et costvmas de Bearn. Pav, J. Desbaratz, 1682. 138 p.

Bordeaux

The ancienne coutume of Bordeaux dates from the thirteenth century. On January 15, 1520, Francis I sent letters patent to François de Belcier, then first president at Bordeaux, ordering the codification of the coutume. The work was not completed until 1527.[8]

1538
500 Arnoldi Ferroni Regii consiliarii in posteriorem partem constitutionum Burdigalensium Commentarij. Lvgdvni, Seb. Gryphivm, 1538. 135 p.

1540
501 Arnoldi Ferroni in consvetvdines Bvrdigalensivm libri II . . . Lvgdvni, Apud S. Gryphivm, 1540. 2 v. in 1.

1593
502 Les anciens statvts de la ville et cite de Bovrdeavs . . . Bovrdeavs, S. Millanges, 1593. 387 p.
   Edited by Gabriel de Lurbe.

1621
503 Commentaire svr les covstvmes generalles de la ville de Bovrdeavs, et pays bovrdelois, par Bernard Avtomne . . . Bovrdeavs, I. Millanges, 1621. 672 p.

1666
504 Commentaire svr les covstvmes generales de la ville de Bovrdeavx, et pays bovrdelois, par Bernard Avthomne . . . Bovrdeavx, Pierre de Coq, 1666. 670 p.

1666
505 Arrests notables dv parlement de Bovrdeavx svr la Covstvme dv pays bovrdelois . . . par Antoine Boé. Bovrdeavx, I. M. Millanges, 1666. 48 p.

1728
506 Commentaire sur les Coûtumes generales de la ville de Bordeaux et Pays Bourdelois. Par feu Bernard Automne . . . mis en abregé . . . par Antoine Boé . . . Révüs . . . par Pierre Dupin . . . Bordeaux, Etienne Labottiere, 1728. 540 p.

1737
507 Commentaire sur les coutumes generales de la ville de Bordeaux et pays bourdelois, par Bernard Automne . . . mis en abregé par Antoine Boé. Rév., corr. & augm. . . . par Pierre Dupin. Derniere ed. avec la révision . . . de Ledoulx & Beaune. Bordeaux, La Compagnie des imprimeurs & libraires, 1737. 540 p.

1746
508 Conference de toutes les questions traitées par de Ferron . . . dans son Commentaire sur la coutume de Bordeaux . . . Avec le Commentaire de Bernard Automne . . . Par feu Pierre Dupin . . . Bordeaux, J. B. Lacornée, 1746. 399 p.

1768–69
509 Coutumes du ressort du Parlement de Guienne; avec un commentaire . . . Bordeaux, Chez les Freres Labottiere, 1768–69. 2 v.

Microfilm: 1540, 1565, 1585, 1621, 1666.

Castel-Amouroux

1888
510 Coutumes de Castel-Amouroux et de Saint-Pastour en Agenais, par H. Emile Rébouis. Paris, L. Larose et Forcel, 1888. 28 p.

Castelsagrat

1887
511 Coutumes de Castelsagrat en Querci. Par H.-Emile Rébouis. Paris, L. Larose et Forcel, 1887. 40 p.

Dauphiné

The Dauphiné, an ancient part of the realms of Burgundy and Arles, was given in 1349 to the house of France by a treaty between the dauphin, Humbert II (1313–1355), and Philip VI of Valois. This statute of 1349 remained the basis of the law of Dauphiné.[9]

1531
512 Statvta Delphinalia . . . Statutz dv Davlphine nouuellement faictz par la supreme court du parlement du daulphine et translates de latin en francoys . . . Grenoble, Bonin Baljarin, 1531. 9 l.

Laroque-Timbaut

1865
513 Coutumes de Larroque-Timbaud, 1270, par A. Moullié. Paris, A. Durand, 1865. 103 p.

Prayssas

1860
514 Coutumes de Prayssas [édité] par A. Moulliez. Paris, Auguste Durand, 1860. 28 p.

Provence

In Provence, Roman law had the character of common law. The counts of Provence and Forcalquier had statutes and ordinances compiled to apply to all of the county of Provence. The first statutes were those of Raymond Bérenger, of the house of Barcelone, drawn up in 1235 to put an end to disagreements between the count and certain lords. In 1243 other statutes, known as *Constitutiones curiae aquensis*, organized the administration of justice in the county. Two years later, in 1245, Provence passed into the power of Charles of Anjou, brother of Louis IX, through the marriage of Béatrix, daughter and heiress of Raymond Bérenger.

Sometime between 1246 and 1285, the first count of the house of Anjou gave a general ordinance de officialibus on the rights of the suzerain which caused a revolution in the order of justice. The city jurisdictions lost their independence, as did the lords. All power was concentrated in the hands of the count, represented by a sénéchal and by lesser magistrates. Barons no longer had the right to dispense justice. After years of discontent, several statutes were published. The most important of these was the 1304 *Statut* compiled by P. Ferrière, archbishop of Arles and chancellor of the realm of Sicily, which dealt with the reformation of Provence and regulated administration, justice, and the police. It was confirmed in 1306 by Robert, eldest son of Charles II and grandson and deputy general of Charles I.

Numerous statutes were compiled during the fourteenth and fifteenth centuries. They were collected as the *Statuts de Provence et de Forcalquier*, which contained edicts from the year 1366 until 1481, the date of the union of Provence with the French crown.[10]

1620
515 Statvts et covstvmes dv pays de Provence. Avec les gloses de L. Masse . . . & d'autres meslanges tres-vtiles aux experts & estimateurs, par I. de Bomy. Aix, Iean Tholosan, 1620. 255 p.

1642
516 Les statvts et covstvmes dv pays de Provence. *Commentées* par Iacqves Morgves . . . Aix, Charles David, 1658. 450 p.

1658
517 Les statvts et covstvmes dv pays de Provence. Commentées par Iacqves Morgves . . . Aix, Charles David, 1658. 450 p.

1665
518 Recveil de qvelqves covstvmes dv pays de Provence . . . par Iean de Bomy . . . Reueu & corrigé . . . Aix, Charles David, 1665. 466 p.

1709
519 Recueil de quelques coutumes du pays de Provence . . . par Jean de Bomy. Revû & corrigé . . . Aix, Antoine David, 1709. 71 p.

Microfilm: 1620, 1642.

Roussillon

Roussillon was ruled in the Middle Ages by the law of the Visigoths and the usages of Barcelona. In 1137, the county of Roussillon passed into the authority of the counts of Barcelona, and the usages of that city retained their vigor.[11]

1893
520 Les infames dans l'ancien droit roussillonnais . . . [par] Emile Desplanque. Perpignan, Charles Latrobe, 1893. 142 p.

Saint-Gauzens

1929 (?)
521 Coutumes du bourg de Saint-Gauzens, Tarn, fondé le 20 février 1270, par Amaury, vicomte de Lautrec. Toulouse, Douladoure Frères [1929?] 39 p.

Saint-Jean-d'Angély[12]

In 1199 Jean sans Terre (John Lackland, king of England, 1199–1216) conceded to Saint-Jean-d'Angély a charter, which was confirmed by Philip Augustus in 1204. The commune of Saint-Jean-d'Angély received many royal confirmations of its privileges.

Before the official codification in 1520 of the coutume of Saintonge (which was called the coutume of Saint-Jean-d'Angély because it was decreed and published in that city), there already existed some private coutumiers. One of these, written by a sénéchal, viscount of Rouchechouard, served as the basis for the deliberations of the commissioners charged with preparing the official codification.[13]

Except for certain regions which were under droit écrit, all of the northern part of the Saintonge, especially the large part of the territory on the left bank of the Charente,[14] observed the coutume of Saintonge.

1638
522 Paraphrasis ad consvetvdinem Santangeliacam. Authore D. Iacobo Vigneo. Santonis, apud Ioannem Bichon, 1638. 328 p.

1647
523 L'vsance de Saintonge . . . 2. ed. Avgmentée . . . par Cosme Bechet. Saintes, Iean Bichon, 1647. 502 p.

1650
524 Commentaires svr la covstvme de Sainct Iean d'Angely composez par le sievr Maichin. S. Iean d'Angely, Pavl d'Angycovrt, 1650. 379, 17 p.

1687
525 Conference de l'usance de Saintes avec la coutume de Saint Jean d'Angely . . . Par Cosme Bechet. 2. ed. Saintes, Estienne Bichon, 1687. 112 p.

1689
526 Coutume du siege royal de St. Jean d'Angely en Saintonge . . . Interpretée et commentée par Cosme Bechet. Saintes, Estienne Bichon, 1689. 356 p.

1701
527 L'usance de Saintogne entre mer et Charente, colligée des anciens manuscrits . . . 3. éd., augm. de nouvelles notes . . . Par Cosme Bechet . . . Bordeaux, Simon Boé, 1701. 394 p.

1708
528 Commentaires sur la coûtume de St. Jean d'Angely. Composez par le Sieur Maichin . . . 2. ed. . . . Saintes, Theodore Delpech, 1708. 386 p.

Microfilm: 1633, 1644.

Toulouse

In the country of Toulouse, Roman law was observed above all, but it was modified by local coutumes, and feudal law was also applied. In the city of Toulouse, the citizen was always master; feudalism predominated only in the surrounding territory.

On March 8, 1216, Simon de Montfort, count of Leicester (1165–1218), took an oath to respect the anciennes coutumes and institutions of Toulouse. In 1283, Philip III (the Bold) confirmed the coutume of Toulouse as compiled and presented to him, and in 1285 King Philip IV (the Fair) also confirmed the coutume, minus twenty articles.[15]
See also Normandy, no. 266 (1513).

1544
529 Consvetvdines Tolosae, cvm declarationibvs in quibus consuetudines . . . Tolosae, Antonij Vincentij, Apud Ludouicum Yuernaige. Impressum per Anthonium Gorcium, 1544. 73 l.

1770
530 Coutumes de la ville, gardiage et viguerie de

Toulouse, en latin et en français . . . par Jean-Antoine Soulatges. Toulouse, Dupleix & Laporte, 1770. 228 p.

1846

531 Las ordenansas et coustumas del Libre Blanc, obseruadas de tota ancianetat, compausadas per las sabias femnas de Tolosa . . . Imprimadas nouuellament a Tolosa, per Iac. Co-lomies, 1555. Réimprimées, Paris, Techener; Toulouse, Delboy, 1846. 36 p.

1886

532 Le droit privé au XIII. [treizième] siècle: d'après les coutumes de Toulouse et de Montpellier, par Adolphe Tardif. Réimpr. de l'ed. de Paris, 1886. Aalen, Scientia-Verlag, 1974. 109 p.

Notes

1. Ernest D. Glasson, *Histoire du droit et des institutions de la France,* 8 vols. (Paris: F. Pichon, 1891), 4: 57.
2. Ibid., p. 106.
3. Ibid., pp. 92–94.
4. Ibid., p. 85.
5. Pierre Barbier, *La Coutume privée d'Andorre* (Paris: A. Rousseau, 1938), pp. 61–62.
6. Glasson, 4: 88.
7. Klimrath, p. 18.
8. *Coutumes du ressort du Parlement de Guienne* (Bordeaux: Chez les freres Labottiere, 1768–69).
9. Glasson, 4: 58.
10. Ibid., pp. 62–65.
11. Ibid., pp. 81–82.
12. Glasson places Saint-Jean-d'Angély in the southern region in vol. 4, in the western region in vol. 8.
13. Glasson, 4: 103–5.
14. Ibid., 8: 80.
15. Ibid., 4: 72.

Appendixes
Glossary of Geographic Terms

Listed below are archaic and variant forms of geographic terms
as they appear in the titles of the coutumes. Numbers refer to
entries.

Agenais—Agen, 494, 495, 510
Andegauensis—Anjou, 200
Andivm—Anjou, 202
Aniov—Anjou, 203, 204
Aruerniae—Auvergne, 48, 49
Arvernorum—Auvergne, 53
Arvernorvm—Auvergne, 47
Aurelianas—Orléanais, 125
Aurelianeñ—Orléans, 71
Aurelianenses—Orléanais, 73
Aurelianorum—Orléanais, 74
Auuergne—Auvergne, 51
Avcerre—Auxerre, 60
Avrelianensis—Orléanais, 76
Avvergne—Auvergne, 52, 54

Bearn—Béarn, 498, 499
Beauuoisis—Beauvaisis, 184
Beauvoisis—Beauvaisis, 65, 66
Beavvaisis—Beauvaisis, 64
Berri—Berry, 80, 82
Bituricēn—Berry, 71
Bituricēses—Berry, 73
Biturigū—Berry, 70
Biturigum—Berry, 72
Bitvricensis—Berry, 76
Bitvrigvm—Berry, 74
Blesenses—Blois, 85
Bourbonnois—Bourbonnais, 30, 89–94
Bourgögne—Burgundy, 407, 410, 427–431, 433–437, 439
Bourgongne—Burgundy, 416
Bovrbonnois—Bourbonnais, 88
Bovrdeavs—Bordeaux, 502, 503
Bovrdeavx—Bordeaux, 504, 505
Bovrgongne—Burgundy, 412, 420–423, 425, 448, 449
Bretaigne—Brittany, 209, 210, 229, 239
Britanniae—Brittany, 216, 218, 221, 224, 227, 233, 234
Britonum—Brittany, 234
Britonvm—Brittany, 214, 216, 218, 221, 224, 227, 233
Buillon—Bouillon, 343
Burdigalensium—Bordeaux, 500
Burgūdie—Burgundy, 408
Burgundiae—Burgundy, 431
Burgundie—Burgundy, 410

Bvillon—Bouillon, 343
Bvrbonias—Bourbonnais, 87
Bvrdigalensivm—Bordeaux, 415, 501
Bvrgvndiae—Burgundy, 411, 413, 414, 417–419, 424, 426

Cambray—Cambrai, 344, 380, 382
Cambresis—Cambrai, 344
Chaalons—Châlons, 346–349, 397
Chalons—Châlons, 401
Champaigne—Champagne, 475
Chaulmont en Bassigny—Chaumont-en-Bassigny, 442, 443
Chaulny—Chauny, 401
Clermont en Beauuoisis—Clermont-en-Beauvaisis, 184

Daniou—Anjou, 198, 199
Daulphine—Dauphiné, 512
Dauuergne—Auvergne, 46
Davlphine—Dauphiné, 512
Delphinalia—Dauphiné, 512
Dorleãs—Orléans, 124

Estampes—Etampes, 100

Flandriae—Flanders, 351
Frãce—France, 3, 4, 7
Franche-conte—Franche-Comté, 448, 449

Grand Perche—Perche, 181–183
Guysnes—Guînes, 358

Haynault—Hainaut, 359
Haynaut—Hainaut, 364
Haynnav—Hainaut, 360–362

Larroque-Timbaud—Laroque-Timbaut, 513
Liege—Liège, 380, 382
Lodunoys—Loudun, 250
Lorryz—Lorris, 124
Lovdvnois—Loudun, 251

Mante—Mantes, 108
Meaulx—Meaux, 1
Montfort-Lamaulry—Montfort-l'Amaury, 114, 115

Niuernois—Nivernais, 121
Nivernois—Nivernais, 116–122
Normaniae—Normandy, 272
Normendie—Normandy, 265, 267, 270, 271, 274

Orleans—Orléans, 1, 126–131

Parisiensis—Paris, 136, 137, 266
Parisiorvm—Paris, 142, 147
Picardie—Picardy, 385, 386
Pictonum—Poitou, 311, 315, 318
Pictonvm—Poitou, 313
Poictou—Poitou, 312, 320, 324
Poictov—Poitou, 314, 316

Rheims—Reims, 389, 397, 401

Sainct Iean d'Angely—Saint-Jean-d'Angély, 524
Santangeliacam—Saint-Jean-d'Angély, 522

Tholosani—Toulouse, 266
Tolosa—Toulouse, 531
Tolosae—Toulouse, 529
Tournay—Tournai, 380, 382, 395
Touronensis—Touraine, 188
Tovraine—Tours, 190
Troies—Troyes, 106
Turoneñ—Tours, 71
Turonum—Tours, 74
Turonenses—Tours, 73
Turonensis—Tours, 188
Tvronensis—Tours, 76

Verdvn—Verdun, 483
Vermendois—Vermandois, 402
Victry—Vitry-en-Parthois, 1
Vlaenderen—Flanders, 350, 352
Vitry en Pertois—Vitry-en-Parthois, 486, 487

Rulers of France 751–1852

Carolingian Dynasty

Pepin III the Short 751–768
Carloman (joint ruler) 768–771
Charlemagne (joint ruler, 768–771) 768–814
Louis I the Pious 814–840
Charles II the Bald 840–877
Louis II 877–879
Louis III (joint ruler) 879–882
Carloman (joint ruler, 879–882) 879–884
Charles the Fat 885–887
Odo, or Eudes (joint ruler, 893–898; non-Carolingian) 888–898
Charles III the Simple (joint ruler, 893–898, 922–923) 893–923
Robert I (joint ruler; non-Carolingian) 922–923
Rudolf (of Burgundy; non-Carolingian) 923–936
Louis IV 936–954
Lothair 954–986
Louis V 986–987

Capetian Dynasty

Hugh Capet 987–996
Robert II 996–1031
Henry I 1031–1060
Philip I 1060–1108
Louis VI 1108–1137
Louis VII 1137–1180
Philip II Augustus 1180–1223
Louis VIII 1223–1226
Louis IX (St. Louis) 1226–1270
Philip III 1270–1285
Philip IV the Fair 1285–1314
Louis X 1314–1316
John I (never reigned)
Philip V 1316–1322
Charles IV 1322–1328

Valois Dynasty

Philip VI 1328–1350
John II the Good 1350–1364

Charles V 1364–1380
Charles VI 1380–1422
Charles VII 1422–1461
Louis XI 1461–1483
Charles VIII 1483–1498
Louis XII 1498–1515
Francis I 1515–1547
Henry II 1547–1559
Francis II 1559–1560
Charles IX 1560–1574
Henry III 1574–1589

Bourbon Dynasty

Henry IV 1589–1610
Louis XIII 1610–1643
Louis XIV 1643–1715
Louis XV 1715–1774
Louis XVI 1774–1792
Louis XVII (never reigned)

First Republic

National Convention 1792–1795
Directory 1795–1799
Consulate 1799–1804

First Empire

Napoleon I 1804–1814, 1815
Napoleon II (never reigned)

Bourbon Dynasty (restored)

Louis XVIII 1814–1824
Charles X 1824–1830

House of Orléans

Louis Philippe 1830–1848

Second Republic

Louis Napoleon, President 1848–1852

Emperors of the Holy Roman Empire

Carolingian Emperors

Charlemagne 800–814
Louis I the Pious 814–840
Lothair I 840–855
Louis II 855–875
Charles II the Bald 875–877
Charles III the Fat 881–887

Emperors from Various Houses

Guy of Spoleto 891–894
Lambert 892–898
Arnulf 896–899
Louis III 901–905
Berengar 915–924

Saxon Emperors

Otto I the Great 962–973
Otto II 973–983
Otto III 983–1002
Henry II 1002–1024

Franconian Emperors (Salian)

Conrad II 1024–1039
Henry III 1039–1056
Henry IV 1056–1106
Henry V 1106–1125

Saxon Emperor

Lothair II 1125–1137

Hohenstaufen Emperors

Conrad III 1138–1152
Frederick I Barbarossa 1152–1190
Henry VI 1190–1197
Philip of Swabia 1198–1208
Otto IV of Brunswick 1198–1215
Frederick II 1212–1250
Conrad IV 1250–1254

The Great Interregnum (1254–1273)
Emperors from Various Houses

Rudolf I of Habsburg 1273–1291
Adolf of Nassau 1292–1298
Albert I of Austria 1298–1308
Henry VII of Luxemburg 1308–1313
Louis IV of Bavaria 1314–1347
Charles IV of Luxemburg 1347–1378
Wenceslaus of Bohemia 1378–1400
Rupert of the Palatinate 1400–1410
Sigismund of Luxemburg 1411–1437

Hapsburg Emperors

Albert II 1438–1439
Frederick III 1440–1493
Maximilian I 1493–1519
Charles V 1519–1556
Ferdinand I 1556–1564
Maximilian II 1564–1576
Rudolf II 1576–1612
Matthias 1612–1619
Ferdinand II 1619–1637
Ferdinand III 1637–1657
Leopold I 1658–1705
Joseph I 1705–1711
Charles VI 1711–1740

Bavarian Emperor

Charles VII 1742–1745

Hapsburg-Lorraine Emperors

Francis I 1745–1765
Joseph II 1765–1790
Leopold II 1790–1792
Francis II 1792–1806

Selected Bibliography

Anderson, Ernst. The renaissance of legal science after the Middle Ages. Copenhagen, Jurist forbundets Forlag, 1974.

Berroyer, Claude. Bibliothèque des coutumes. Paris, Nicolas Gosselin, 1699.

Besnier, Robert. La Coutume de Normandie, histoire externe. Paris, Librairie du Recueil Sirey, 1935.

Bourdot de Richebourg, Charles Antoine. Nouveau Coutumier general, ou Corps des coutumes generales et particulieres de France. Paris, T. Le Gras, 1724.

Chénon, Emile. Le "Pays" de Berry et le "dédroit" de sa coutume. Paris, F. Pichon, 1891.

La Grande Encyclopédie. Paris, H. Lamirault & Cie, 1886–1902.

Filhol, René. Le Vieux Coutumier de Poictou. Bourges, Editions Tardy, 1956.

Glasson, Ernest Désiré. Histoire du droit et des institutions de la France. Paris, F. Pichon, 1891.

Klimrath, Henri. Etudes sur les coutumes. Paris, Levrault, 1837.

Lebrun, Auguste. La Coutume, ses sources—son authorité en droit privé. Paris, R. Pichon et R. Durand-Auzias, 1932.

Lefebvre, Maurice. La Coutume comme source formalle de droit. Lille, Camilla Robbe, 1906.

Salmon, Amédée. Coutumes de Beauvaisis. Paris, A. et J. Picard, 1970–74.

Tardif, Ernest-Joseph. Coutumiers de Normandie. Rouen, Imprimerie de Espérance Cagniard, 1881. vol. 1.

Tardif, Ernest-Joseph. Coutumiers de Normandie. Rouen, A. Lestringaut; Paris, A. Picard et fils, 1896. vol. 2.

Tardif, Ernest-Joseph. Les Auteurs présumés du Grand coutumier de Normandie. Paris, L. Larose et Forcel, 1885.

Testaud, Georges. La Coutume du comté de Clermont-en-Beauvaisis de 1496. Paris, Librairie de la Société du Recueil Gal des lois et des arrêts, 1903.

Indexes

Names Cited in the Text

Numbers refer to pages.

Ableiges, Jacques d', 7
Alençon, duke of, 25
Anne of France, duchess of Bourbonnais, 17
Argentré, Bertrand d', 30
Aumery, Jean, 44

Baillet, Thibault, 17, 22, 26, 29, 33, 38, 54, 56, 57, 58
Barme, Roger, 17, 29, 33, 38, 57, 58
Baudouin II, 44
Beaune, Henri, 7
Belcier, François de, 62
Bérenger, Raymond, 63
Berlaymont, Louis de, 43
Berroyer, Claude, 7
Besançon, de, 17, 46, 56
Billon, Edme, 14
Bohier, Nicolas de, 19
Bourdin, Jacques, 18, 19, 20, 48
Bourdot de Richebourg, Charles Antoine, 42
Bourgoin, Guillaume, 21
Boutillier, Jean, 7
Boutin, Jacques, 38
Brachet, Nicole, 17
Burdelot, 26
Buynard, Etienne, 21

Carmone, 46
Celestin III, 22
Chambellan, David, 15
Charles II, 63
Charles III, 55, 57, 63
Charles IV, 57
Charles V, 43, 44, 45, 46
Charles VI, 7
Charles VII, 3, 16, 18, 19, 26
Charles VIII, 3, 13, 19, 20
Charles IX, 14, 55, 56, 57
Charles, duke of Bourbonnais, 17
Clermont, count of, 17
Cliton, Guillaume, 47

Dany, Blanchet, 14
Dareste, Rodolphe, 7
Delisle, Léopold, 7

Duprat, Antoine, 13
Dupré, Nicholas, 44

Egenolphe III, 56

Faber, Jean, 29
Faye, Barthélemy, 14, 18, 19, 20, 26, 38, 41, 48
Ferdinand, bishop of Liège and duke of Bouillon, 42
Francis I, 16, 17, 19, 20, 30, 33, 62
François II, 20, 29, 33

Glasson, Ernest Désiré, 3, 4, 14
Guillard, André, 15, 25
Guillaume II, 56
Guy, count, 41

Henry II, 14, 20, 29, 33, 44, 62
Henry III, 21, 30, 55
Henry IV, 35, 55
Henry, duke of Lorraine and Bar, 56
Humbert II, 63

Isabelle of Haynaut, 42

Jaquelline of Holland, 44
Jean, duke of Berry, 7

Laboulaye, Edouard, 7
La Chaussée, Jehan de, 38
Lambertière, Jehan de, 38
La Mothe, Charles de, 33
Leicester, count of, 64
Lelièvre, Jean, 29, 33
Le Viste, Antoine, 17
Lizet, Pierre, 16
Louis VI, 18
Louis VII, 18, 25
Louis IX, 41, 63
Louis XI, 18, 26
Louis XII, 13, 14, 17, 19, 20, 21, 22, 33, 38
Louis XIII, 18, 55

Mathé, Pierre, 16
Maximilian, emperor, 44
Maximin II, 56
Montferrand, 13
Montfort, Simon de, 22, 64
Moysen, Loyset, 38

Napoleon, 4

Philip I, of Castile, 44
Philip II, Augustus, 18, 19, 26, 41, 42, 64
Philip III, the Bold, 64
Philip VI, 63
Philip the Good, duke of Burgundy, 4, 52
Philip IV, of Spain, the Fair, 45, 64
Philippe de Remi, sire de Beaumanoir, 3, 15
Picot, 13
Pierre II, duke of Bourbonnais, 17
Poigne, Pierre, 38

Ribeaupierre, 56
Richebourg Saint Vasst, lord of, 42
Robert, count of Artois, 42, 63
Robert, count of France, 15
Robert de la Marck, Henry, 47
Roiger, Guillaume, 21
Roisin, Jean, 45
Rouillard, Louis, 21

Thaumas de la Thaumassière, Gaspard, sieur du Puy-Ferrand,
   15, 16
Thibault, Nicole, 15, 25
Thou, Christofle de, 14, 18, 19, 20, 22, 26, 38, 41, 48
Tutant, Robert, 38

Viole, Jacques, 14, 26, 38, 41, 48

Yves, count, 41

Author and Compiler Index

Numbers refer to entries.

Ableiges, Jacques d' (fl. 1371–1391), 12, 36, 44
Amaury, Vicomte de Lautrec, 521
Andre, Jehan; *see* Andreae, Joannes
Andreae, Joannes (d. 1348), 265
Angevin, Gabriel Michel; *see* Michel de La Rochemaillet, Gabriel
Angleberme, Jean Pyrrhus d' (ca. 1470–1521), 71, 73, 74, 76, 125
Anjorrant, Claude, 139
Ansart, Robert, 338
Aramon, Sauvan d'; *see* Sauvan d'Aramon
Argentré, Bertrand d' (1519–1590), 212–216, 218, 219, 221, 222, 224–226, 228, 232–234, 243
Argentré, Charles d' [Caroli de] (fl. 1610), 216, 221, 224
Aufreri, Etienne (d. 1511), 266
Aufrerij, Stephani; *see* Aufreri, Etienne
Auroux Des Pommiers, Matthieu (fl. 1730), 90–94
Automne, Bernard (d. 1666), 503, 504, 506–508
Aviron; *see* Le Batelier d'Aviron, Jacques
Avthomne, Bernard; *see* Automne, Bernard
Avtomne, Bernard; *see* Automne, Bernard

Baillet, Thibault, 187, 199
Bannelier, Jean (1683–1766), 437
Barbier, Pierre, 463, 496, 497
Barraud, Jacques, 316
Basmaison-Pougnet, Jean de (ca. 1535–1594), 50, 52, 54
Basnage, Henri [Henry], sieur de Franquenay (1615–1695), 285, 289
Beaumanoir, Philippe[s] de; *see* Philippe de Remi, sire de Beaumanoir
Beaune, Henri François Bénigne (b. 1833), 37–40, 507
Beautemps-Beaupré, Charles Jean (1823–1899), 402
Bechet, Cosme (fl. 1675), 523, 525–527
Bégat, Jean Baptiste Agneau (1523–1572), 425, 428, 430, 436
Belordeau, Pierre (fl. 1598–1624), 217, 220, 223, 231
Bérault, Josias (1563–ca. 1640), 280, 282–284, 294, 301
Berroyer, Claude (1655–1735), 30, 159, 162, 170, 287
Besnier, Robert, 310
Bessian, Jean, 46, 53
Bessiani, Ioannis [Joannis]; *see* Bessian, Jean
Beugnot, Arthur Auguste, comte (1797–1865), 66
Bevy, Joly de, 438
Biarnoy de Merville, Pierre (d. 1740); *see* Merville, Pierre Biarnoy de
Billecart, Loüis, 349, 401
Billon, Edme, 62
Blécourt, Anne Siberdinus de (b. 1873), 345
Bobé, Jean, 111
Bodreau, Julien (ca. 1599–1664), 256, 257, 259
Boé, Antoine, 505–507
Boerij, Nicolaü; *see* Bohier, Nicolas de
Boerius, Nicolaus; *see* Bohier, Nicolas de
Boguet, Henri (fl. 1603), 418, 432
Boguetus, Henricus; *see* Boguet, Henri
Bohier, Nicolas de (1469–1539), 70–74, 76
Boiceau, Jean, sieur de la Borderie (1513–1591), 318
Bomy, Jean de [I. de], 515, 518, 519
Bonvalot, Edouard Théodore (b. 1825), 447, 457, 468
Bosselli, Io.; *see* Boiceau, Jean
Bottelgier, Jan; *see* Boutillier, Jean

Bouchel, Laurent (1559–1629), 184, 186
Boucheul, Joseph (d. 1706), 321
Bouhier, Jean (1673–1746), 434, 438
Bourdot, Charles A.; *see* Bourdot de Richebourg, Charles Antoine
Bourdot de Richebourg, Charles Antoine (1665–1735), 33
Bourgogne, Nicolas de (1586–1649), 351
Bourjon, François (d. 1751), 169, 174
Bouthors, Alesandre (1797–1869), 332
Boutillier, Jean [Jehan], 5, 6, 13, 23
Bouvot, J., 412, 420, 421
Bovck, Iean le, 368
Bovteiller, Iean; *see* Boutillier, Jean
Bovvet, I.; *see* Bouvot, J.
Bretagne, François (1608–1687), 433
Bri; *see* Bry, Gilles
Brodeau, Julien (d. 1653), 33, 56, 57, 151, 155, 156
Brun-Lavainne, 375
Buche, H., 178
Burdelot, Jehan, 187
Burgundus, Nicolaus; *see* Bourgogne, Nicolas de
Buridan, Jean Baptiste de (d. 1633), 389, 399, 401

Caballinus, Gaspar; *see* Du Moulin, Charles
Canon, Pierre, 451
Caron, Lovys Charondas le; *see* Le Caron, Loys Charondas
Chabrol, Guillaume Michel (1714–1792), 57, 58
Challine, Paul, 27, 34
Champeaux, Ernest (b. 1870), 439
Champy, I., 110
Chartier, Mathieu, 139
Chassenaeus, Bartholomaeus à; *see* Chasseneuz, Barthélemy de
Chasseneuz, Barthélemy de (1480–1541), 408–411, 413, 414, 417, 419, 424, 426, 428, 436
Chauvelin, Toussaint, 33, 56, 57
Chemin, Michel du, 330
Chénon, Emile [i.e., Paul Philippe Joseph Emile Chénon] (1857–1927), 84, 262
Chenouteau, Pelée de, 474
Choppin, René (1537–1606), 142, 147, 149, 152, 202
Choppini, Renati; *see* Choppin, René
Collet, Philibert (1643–1718), 405
Constant, Jean, seigneur des Chézeaux (1589?–1652), 318
Constantii, Ioan; *see* Constant, Jean
Consvl, Gvillavme; *see* Gvillavme, Consvl
Contius, Antonius; *see* Le Conte, Antoine
Coquille, Guy (1523–1603), 15, 17, 20, 25, 116–121, 123
Cornuel, 339
Couart, J., 96, 98
Coudert, Jean Joseph Henri, 481
Courtois, Aimé (1811–1864), 358
Cousin, Ch., 394

D**, G**, 177
Dareste de La Chavanne, Rodolphe (1824–1911), 36, 44
D'Aviron; *see* Le Batelier d'Aviron, Jacques
Davot, Gabriel (1677–1742), 437
Delalande, Jacques; *see* La Lande, Jacques
Delommeau, Pierre, 201
Denisart, Jean Baptiste (1713–1765), 171
Depringles, I.; *see* Despringles, Jean

Descousu, Hugues, 420
Des Maisons, François C. (fl. 1660), 154
Desplanque, Emile Alexandre Joseph (b. 1865), 520
Despringles, Jean (1550–1629), 425, 428, 430, 436
Dilange, Nicolaus (b. 1666), 463
Dolano, Henrico Bogveto; *see* Boguet, Henri
Dubours, 385
Ducastel, Jean Baptiste Louis (1740–1799), 304
Ducros, Jacques (fl. 1658), 493
Dufresne, Jean (d. 1675), 326, 385
Dumées, Antoine François Joseph, 363
Du Molin, Charles; *see* Du Moulin, Charles
Du Moulin, Charles (1500–1566), 9, 14, 21, 22, 24, 28, 30, 32, 33, 50, 52, 54–57, 85, 88–90, 92, 95, 96, 103–106, 110, 130, 136, 137, 150, 153, 157, 194, 205, 206, 243, 257, 314, 321, 327, 332, 425, 428, 436, 486, 487
Dumoulin, Charles; *see* Du Moulin, Charles
Dunod, 435
Dupin, André Marie Jean Jacques (1783–1865), 35, 123
Dupin, Charles, baron [Baron Pierre Charles François Dupin] (1784–1873), 35, 123
Dupin, Pierre (1681–1745), 506–508
Du Pineau, Gabriel (1573–1644), 205, 206
Duplessis, Claude, 159, 162, 170, 260
Du Pont, Denys, 85
Durand, Etienne [Estienne], 490
Duret, Jean (ca. 1540–1606), 90, 92, 94, 127
Dv Fresne, Jean; *see* Dufresne, Jean
Dv Molin, C.; *see* Du Moulin, Charles

Englebermeus, Jonnes Pyrrhus; *see* Angleberme, Jean Pyrrhus
Everard, Etienne [Estienne], 286

Fabert, Abraham, 452
Faye, Barthélemy, seigneur d'Espeisses, 108, 312, 346, 348, 388, 398
Ferrière, Claude de (1639–1715), 29, 158, 161, 163–165, 172, 173, 176
Ferrière, Claude Joseph de, 163, 164
Ferroni, Arnoldi; *see* Le Ferron, Arnoul
Filhol, René, 324
Filleau de La Chaise, Jean (ca. 1630–1693), 319, 320
Fornier, Henry, 130
Fortin, G., 150
Fortius, 361, 362
Fournoue, Couturier de, 109
Fourré, 86
Frère, Edouard Benjamin (1797–1874), 306
Frerot, Nicolas M., 95
Furic, Julien, 226

Gandillaud, Pierre, sieur de Fronfroide (fl. 1598), 193, 194
Garnich, Jacob, 456
Genenois, Gabriel le, 441, 443
Gillisen, John, 42
Godefroy, Denis (1549–1621), 76
Godefroy, Jacques (1587–1652), 281, 284, 301
Godet, Louis [Lovys], sieur de Thilloy (b. 1588), 347, 401
Gosset, 385
Gothofredus, Dionysius; *see* Godefroy, Denis
Gousset, Jean, 441, 442, 444
Gräfe, Reinald, 45
Grimavdet, Francois; *see* Grimmaudet, François
Grimmaudet, François, 10
Guénois, Pierre (ca. 1500–1600), 11
Guillard, André, 107
Guillaume, Jean, 430

Gvenoys, Pierre; *see* Guénois, Pierre
Gvillavme, Consvl, 54
Gyves, ——— de, 129

Hane, Laureyns [Laurens] vanden, 350, 352, 353
Harcher, Jean Baptiste Louis (1700–1753), 322
Harley, Achille[s] de (1536–1610), 126
Héricourt du Vatier, Louis de (1687–1752), 401
Heu, A.; *see* Hev, Adrien de
Hev, Adrien de, 325, 385
Hévin, Pierre (1621–1692), 241, 243

Ibelin, Jean d', comte de Jaffa et d'Ascalon (d. 1266), 65
Iobelot, 407
Ioly, Iacq.; *see* Joly, Jacques

Jacquet, 191
Jehan le lieur, 199, 252
Jehannin, François Claude (1630–1698), 433
Jöcher, 463
Joly, Jacques, 153

Labbé, Charles, 153
Labbé de Monvéron, Gabriel (1582–1657), 75, 77
La Bigotière, René de, seigneur de Perchambault (ca. 1640–1727), 236, 237
Laboulaye, Edouard René Lefebvre de (1811–1883), 35, 36, 44
Lacarrière, Jules, 59
La Fons, Claude de, 400, 401
Laistre, Juste de, 445, 446, 472
La Lande, Jacques de (d. 1703), 128–130
La Mare, Philippe de (1615–1687), 433
Lambert, Guillaume (b. 1520), 272, 275
Lamy, Marc-Antoine, 100
Lançon, Nicolas-François, 466
Laplanche, Jean de, 41
Laurent, Charles (d. 1837), 378, 379
Laurière, Eusèbe Jacob de (1659–1728), 30, 31, 35, 159, 162, 170, 175, 287
La Villette, 385
Le Batelier d'Aviron, Jacques (16th cent.), 294, 301
Le Camus, Jean (1636–1710), 163, 164
Le Caron, Loys [Lovys] Charondas (1536–1617), 12, 13, 23, 140, 141, 143, 144, 385
Lecesne, Edmond (b. 1813), 340
Leclercq, Mathieu Nicolas Joseph (1796–1889), 378
Le Conte, Antoine (1517–1586), 303
Ledoulx, 507
Le Ferron, Arnoul (1515–1563), 415, 500, 501, 508
Le Grand, Louis (1588–1664), 353, 476–479
Leguay, L., 101
Lelet, Jean, 319, 320
Le Lieur; *see* Jehan le lieur
Le Maistre, Pierre; *see* Maistre, Pierre le
Le Page, lieutenant particulier au bailliage de Montargis, 105, 106
Le Paige, Jean, l'aîne (1651–1713), 403
Le Provst, Pierre, 251
Le Rouillé, Guillaume (ca. 1494–1550), 253, 269, 270
Le Royer de la Tournerie, Etienne, 302
Lessaeo, Tanigio Sorino, 272
Leu, S. de, 186
Lhoste, Antoine (fl. 1629), 103, 104, 106
Livonniere, Claude Poquet de, 206
Loisel, Antoine [Anthoine] (1536–1617), 18, 26, 27, 31, 35, 121
Longueil, Pierre de, 139
Louis, Mathurin, 258

Louvet, Pierre, 64
Lovvet, Godet; *see* Godet, Louis
Loysel, Antoine; *see* Loisel, Antoine
Lozembrune, Le Roy de, 386
Lurbe, Gabriel (d. 1613?), 502

M ***, avocat au Parlement, 56, 167, 168, 240, 249, 322, 330
Maichin, 524, 528
Maillart, Adrien, 336, 337
Maistre, Pierre le, 160, 167
Mallet, E., 83
Mallety, Juliani, 426
Marcilly, Laurent, 480
Marnier, Auge Ignace (1786–1861), 305, 386
Marquet, Louis, 323
Martin, Olivier; *see* Olivier-Martin, François Jean Marie
Masse, L., 515
Meijers, Eduard Maurits (b. 1880), 345, 391, 467, 485
Merville, Pierre Biarnoy de (d. 1740), 99, 288, 292, 293
Michel, Gabriel Angevin; *see* Michel de La Rochemaillet, Gabriel
Michel de La Rochemaillet, Gabriel (1561–1642), 14, 21, 22, 24, 28, 33, 152
Migeonis, J., 79
Mingon, François [Frãcisci] (fl. 1530), 200
Molendineus, Carolus; *see* Du Moulin, Charles
Molinaeus, Carolus; *see* Du Moulin, Charles
Monier, Raymond, 376
Morgues, Jacques, 516, 517
Mouillié, Amédée, 513, 514
Moulliez, A.; *see* Mouillié, Amédée

N ***, 298

Olivier de Saint Vast, Louis (b. 1724), 261
Olivier-Martin, François Jean Marie (b. 1879), 179, 180

Pallu, Etienne, 190
Pannier, Victor (1777–1862), 306
Papon, Jean (ca. 1505–1590), 87, 90, 92, 94
Paponis, Ioannis; *see* Papon, Jean
Pasquier, F., 392
Patou, 374
Penon, Jean, 473
Perreaux, Philippe Auguste, 129
Perrier, Nicolas, 433
Pesnelle, N. (fl. 1705), 287, 291, 297, 298
Pétramand, Jean (1580–1621), 449
Philippe de Remi, sire de Beaumanoir (d. 1296), 65–67, 69
Pigornet, Philippe, 196
Pinault des Jaunaux, Matthieu, 344
Pithou, Pierre (1539–1596), 475
Planiol, Marcel Fernand (1853–1931), 247
Pontani, Dionysii; *see* Du Point, Denys
Portejoie, Paulette, 440
Pothier, Robert Joseph (1699–1772), 131–134
Potier, Jacques (ca. 1500–1555), 90, 92, 94
Poullain de Belair, H. E. (1661–1740), 243
Poullain du Parc, Augustin Marie (1703–1782), 243, 244, 246
Pringles, Jean de; *see* Despringles, Jean de
Prohet, Claude-Ignace, 55, 56
Publitium, Aymonem; *see* Publitius, Aymo
Publitius, Aymo, 48, 49

Querard, 463

Ragueau, François (d. 1605), 19, 33
Raparlier, Philippe Joseph, 364

Rat, Pierre [Petri], 311, 315
Rébouis, H.-Emile, 494, 495, 510, 511
Revel, Charles, 406
Ricard, Jean Marie (1622–1678), 33, 56, 57, 185, 186, 327, 331, 385
Riston, Victor, 458
Robert, 192
Rochemaillet, Gabriel-Michel de la; *see* Michel de la Rochemaillet, Gabriel
Roisin, Jean (13th cent.), 375, 376
Roupnel, Jacques Henri (b. 1721), 297, 299
Roupnel de Chenilly; *see* Roupnel, Jacques Henri
Routier, Charles, 295
Rozmar, F. de, 242, 245
Rubys, Claude de, 416

S., T. D., 474
Sainson, Joannes (16th cent.), 73, 74, 76, 188
Sainsonius, Ioan; *see* Sainson, Joannes
Saint-Léger, A. de, 376
Sainxonius, Ioannis; *see* Sainson, Joannes
Salligny, Charles de, 488, 489
Salmon, Amédée (1850–1920), 67, 69
Salverda de Grave, Jean Jacques (1883–1947), 391, 467, 485
Sauvageau, Michel (d. 1712), 238, 239, 242, 245
Sauvan d'Aramon, 172, 176
Schneider, J., 467
Sevenet, Louis Alphonse, 112, 113
Souchet, Etienne, 197
Soulatges, Jean Antoine, 530

T. D. S.; *see* S., T. D.
Taisand, Pierre (1644–1715), 428, 438
Tailliar, Eugene François Joseph (1803–1878), 358
Tardif, Adolphe François Lucien (1824–1890), 107, 341, 532
Tardif, Ernest-Joseph (1855–1922), 307
Testaud, Georges, 68
Thaumas de la Thaumassière, Gaspard, sieur du Puy-Ferrand (d. 1712?), 65, 78, 80–83
Thaumassière, Gaspard Thaumas de la; *see* Thaumas de la Thaumassière, Gaspard
Theveneav, N., 314
Thibault, Nicole, 252
Thou, Christofle [Chrestofle] de (1508–1582), 10, 108, 139, 311, 346, 348, 388, 398
Thourette, Claude, 114, 115
Tiraqueau, André (1480–1558), 313, 314
Tiraqvellus, Andrea; *see* Tiraqueau, André
Tournet, Jean, 148, 153
Tovraille, Pierre, 204
Tronçon, Jean, 145
Trottier, 208
Tvlove, Gilles, 95

Valin, René Josué (1695–1765), 248, 249
Varin, Pierre, 390
Verriest, Léo (b. 1881), 396
Vigier, François, 196
Vigier, Jacques, 196
Vigier, Jean, 195, 196
Vigneo, Iacobo D., 522
Vilade, Léon de, 308
Villers, Philippe de, 430
Viole, Jacques, 108, 139, 312, 346, 348, 388, 398
Vrevin, Louis, 401

Yver, Jean, 43

Printer, Publisher, and Vendor Index

Numbers refer to entries.

Aliot, Gervais; *see* Alliot, Gervais
Allin, Iacobum d', 28, 232, 233
Alliot, A., 256
Alliot, Gervais, 148, 195, 325, 476
Amassard, Michel, 319
Ambroise, A., 451
Angier, Michel, 265
Angycovrt, Pavl, 524
Antoine, Brice, 462, 463, 469; la veuve de, 464, 466
Antoine, François, 484
Antoine, Jean, 470
Augé, A. J. B., 433, 434
Avril, P., 203

Babin, 456
Bacot, A., 146
Bacquenois, N., 397
Bailly, A., 183
Baljarin, Bonin, 512
Barbier, I., 54
Barbier, Paul, 454
Barriere, Louis-Charles, 192, 207
Bart et Held-Baltzinger, 447
Bassaei, Nicolai, 76
Bassée, Nikolaus; *see* Bassaei, Nicolai
Batines, Colomb de, 375
Bauche, Claude Jean-Baptiste, 168
Bechet, D., 151, 155
Bellere, Baltazar, 368
Bernard, M., 404
Bernigaud, 439
Berthelin, D., 284
Besongne, Jean-Baptiste, 290, 291, 294, 296, 298
Bichon, Estienne, 525, 526
Billaine, Lovis, 65, 151, 389
Blaise, Thomas, 103
Bobin, Jerosme, 105, 106, 114
Boé, S., 527
Bogillot, Joan. Cl., 432
Borde, J., 129
Boschman, G., 53
Bouchard, C., 452, 490
Bouchard, François, 377, 400, 460, 461, 483
Bouchetz, frères, 250, 314
Bourgoignon, Philippes, 210
Bovtonné, R., 184
Boyer, Jacques, 81
Braud, Jean Babtiste, 319
Bravd, Eliae, 318
Briard, 300
Briday, 37, 38
Briden, Gabriel, 444
Briguet, 39, 40
Brillard, Ambrois, 75
Buon, Nicolas [Nicolaum; Nicolai], 77, 127, 213, 225, 227, 228

Cagniard, E., 307
Candelarius, Petrus, 272
Carteron, C., 405
Cauellat, G., 10
Cavelier, G., 160

Cellot, 174; *see also* Grangé
Centre lorrain d'histoire de droit, 481, 482
Chanvin, fils, 358
Charpentier, Henri, 99, 100, 288
Chavdiere, G., 11
Chevalier, Pierre, 19, 102, 144
Chouët, Pierre & Iaques, 420
Clousier, Jacques, 115
Clousier, la veuve, 97
Cochart, Jean, 29, 158, 161
Cock, Symon, 6
Cognard, Jean-Baptiste, 206
Coignet-Darnault, 332
Collignon, Joseph, 465
Colomies, Iac., 532
Companie des Libraires, 173
Constant, Nicolas, 487
Courtin, A., 340
Courtois, Robert, 319
Couteau, Gillet, 252
Covterot, E., 152
Cramoisy, Clavde, 118
Crapelet, 390
Crispini, Samuelis, 419, 424
Cristo, Jean Jacques, 80, 82
Cusson, J. B., 455
Cvsset, P., 425

Dallier, I. [Iehan], 108, 181
Dangiers, 199
David, Antoine, 519
David, Charles, 517, 518
David, E., 329, 516
David, Michel, 163
Debure, frères, 132–134
Dégouette, Martin, 57, 58, 94
Delboy, 531
Delhomme & Briquet, 39, 40
Delpech, Theodore, 528
Derbaix, 34, 364
Desbaratz, J., 499
Desbordes, René-Jacob, 248
Des Marescs, Gvillavme, 277
Desventes, F., 436
Devérité, 331
Domat-Montchrestien, 376
Dominique, A., 448, 449
Douilliez, N. J., 353
Douladoure, frères, 521
Duchemin, Edouard, 83
Du Clos, Julien, 211
Dufour, 172
Du Mesnil, Paulus, 90
Dumortier, 374
Du Petit Val, David, 280–283
Du Puis, Gregoire-Antoine, 446
Du Puys, Iacques [Iaques], 9, 138, 139, 272, 275, 276
Dupuys, I.; *see* Du Puys, Iacques
Durand, 35, 105, 106, 308, 447
Durand, A. [Auguste], 36, 306, 402, 468, 513, 514

Gaisne, Iean, 229, 230
Garnice, Iacob, 450
Garnier, François, 60
Garnier, P., 231, 236; la veuve de, 237
Gayav, Iean, 493
Gerard, Anthoine, 187
Gillet, Louis, 320
Gobbaerts, F., 355, 378, 379
Goemaere, J., 396
Gogué, 113
Gorcius, Anthonius, 529
Gosselin, Nicolas, 30, 31, 159, 162, 164, 260, 336
Grabit, J. Sulpice, 176
Graet, Masimiliaen, 350
Grangier, Antoine, 423
Grangé, 169, 174
Griveav, George, 204
Gryphivs, Antonivs, 415
Gryphivs, Seb., 500, 501
Guénégaud, Librairie, 58
Guignard, Jean, 55, 62, 85, 156, 477; le père, 185
Guignard & C. Robustel, 328
Guillyn, 172
Gvillemot, 104
Gvyot, Clavde, 422

Hagius, Joh. Fridericus, 351
Hecart, Nicolas, 399
Henry, J. B., 373
Hérissant, fils, 480
Hervé, L., 247
Hostingne, Laurens, 265
Hotot, F., 128
Hottot, Satvrny, 126
Hovion, Pierre, 443
Hovzé, Iean, 12, 22
Hoys, Iacobi, 125
Hubault, R., veuve de, 327
Hvby, François, 95

Ianot, Denis, 5
Imprimerie de la société de typographie, 101
Imprimerie de Monsieur, 177
Imprimerie Privilégiée, 301–303

Jannot, André, 473
Jouve & Cie, 59
Jovenau, N., 395

Knapen, 191, 301, 330
Knobbaert, M., 352

Labottiere, Etienne, 506, 509
Lacornée, J. B., 508
Lafolye, 262
Lallemant, R., 297, 299
Lamy, Pierre, 150
L'Angelier, A. [Abel], 15–18, 20, 116, 117, 475
L'Angelier, Arnoul [Arnoldum], 8, 48
La Nove, Gvillavme de, 14
Laporte, 530
La Roche, Erneste de, 381, 382
La Roche, Simeon de, 360, 361, 380
Larose, L., et Forcel, 178, 309, 392, 494, 495, 510, 511
La Tovr, E., 190
Latrobe, Charles, 520
Le Blanc, Iean, 275
Le Boucher, Pierre, 295, 303

Le Breton, 92, 93
Le Brument, A., 306
Lechleri, Martini, 417
Lechet, J., 403
Le Febvre, P. Louis, 122
Le Gras, 165
Le Gras, Henry, 26, 27, 121
Le Gras, Theodore, 33, 167
Le Mesgissier, Martin, 271, 274, 278
Le-Mvr, Pierre, 182
Le Preux, Ioannes, 137
Le Preux, Poncet [Poncetum], 49, 136
Le Qvevx, Charles, 384
Leroux, Ernest, 179
Le Roux, Nicolas, 270
L'Hvillier, P., 140, 141
Librairie nouvelle de droit de jurisprudence, 458
Lochet, J., 403
Loy, Jehan, 359
Loyson, G., 119, 120
Lvynes, G. de, 154

Macé, Barthelemy, 13
Mace, Jehan, 265
Mairesse, M., 344
Malassis, J. Z., le jeune, 261
Mame, 208
Mangeant, Iaques, 279
Marechal, J., 408
Mareschal, Jacques, 238, 239
Marnef, H. de, 10
Marnefi Fratres, 311
Masson, J. P. J., 86
Massot, Estienne, 98
Maurry, A., 286, 287, 289; la veuve de, 285
Mavcroy, Estienne, 326
Mesnier, A., 293, 315, 491
Mettayer, I., 140, 141
Migeot, Gaspard, 362
Millanges, I. M., 503, 505
Millanges, S., 502
Moette, Thomas, 157
Moitemont, Jean-Baptiste de, 372
Montalant, 478, 479
Moreav, Denys, 96
Morel, J., 65
Mouchet, Denis [Denys], 32, 445
Musterschmidt-Verlag, 45

Neveu, Durand, 298
Nion, Vrbain, 189
Nobily, G., 347
Nully, Jean de, 170
Nyon, 175

Olivier, Gervais, 255
Olivier, Hierome, 254, 257–259
Ory, Marc, 21
Osmont, frères, 91, 472
Osmont, C., 205
Oudin, P., 440
Oursel, L., 304

Paruo, Ioanne, 200
Paruus, Oudoënus, 74
Pedone-Lauriel, 30, 308, 447, 457
Pepingue, N., 110
Pepingvé, Edme, 25

Petit, Jehan [Jean], 3, 46, 72, 124, 135
Picard, A., 107, 341; et fils, 67
Picard, A. et J., 69
Pissot, Noel, 99
Pillehotte, Ioannem, 418
Plihorn, J., 247
Plon, H., 123
Portau, Thomas, 201, 251
Poussin, Jacques, 188
Poyure, Henry, 498
Pratensi, Galeoto, 73
Prato, Joannes de, 264
Prault, 166
Privat, 439
Puinesge, Maurice, 196

Rache, Nicolas de, 370, 371
Ravoux, J., 406
Regnault, François [Frānciscû; Fracisci; Frāncovs], 2, 71, 253, 268–270, 410
Remelein, 245
Renouard, J., 66
Ressayre, Jean, 427–429
Rezé, Clavde, 194
Rezé, Simon, 196
Richard, Jehan, 267
Richeboys, Gilles, 471
Richer, Estienne, 149
Rigavd, Benoist, 416
Rigavd, Simon, 23
Robbe, C., 356
Robustel, C., 328
Roigny, J. de, 7
Roigny, Michel de, 441
Rousseau, Arthur, 394, 496, 497
Rouy, J., 337
Rouzeau, F., 130
Rouzeau-Montaut, J., 131; veuve, 132–134
Rovillivs, Gvlielmvs, 313

Saint, P. de, 434
Savoye, 171
Scientia Verlag, 44, 532
Seneuze, 492
Seneuze, J., 489
Senevze, Qventin, 488

Sercy, Charles de, 349, 453
Simon, P.-G., 333
Sirey, 41, 43, 84, 180, 310
Sirot, Jean, la veuve de, 437
Sonnius, C., 24
Sonnius, L., 202
Sonnivs, Michaelem [Michel], 142, 147, 193
Sovbron, André, 153
Sovoye, 171
Stammii, Johannis, 235

Tarbé, P. H., 112, 474
Tardy, 324
Téchener, 305, 386, 531
Tholosan, I., 515
Thoreav, Ivlian, 316, 317
Tornaesivs, Ioan, 87
Toubeau, François, 65, 78, 79

Unions des imprimeries (prons), 365, 366
Université libre de Bruxelles, 42

Valet, G., 64
Vanackere, 375
Varret, M., 383
Vatar, F., 246
Vatar, G., 241, 243, 244
Vatar, J. [Jean], 229, 230, 242
Vatard, Pierre, 60
Verger, N., 240
Vernoy, Claude, 89
Viallanes, P., 56, 109
Villery, Maurice, 186
Vincent, 249
Vincent, B., 88
Vincent, Symon, 70, 408
Vincentius, Antonius [Antonij], 47, 411, 529
Vincentius, Bartholomaeus, 413, 414, 426
Vingles, Johan de, 498
Vvinde, Loys de, 367

Willerval, J. F., 363
Willink, H. D. Tjeenk, 345, 391, 467, 485

Yuernaige, Ludouicum, 529

☆ U.S. GOVERNMENT PRINTING OFFICE : 1978 O—243-120

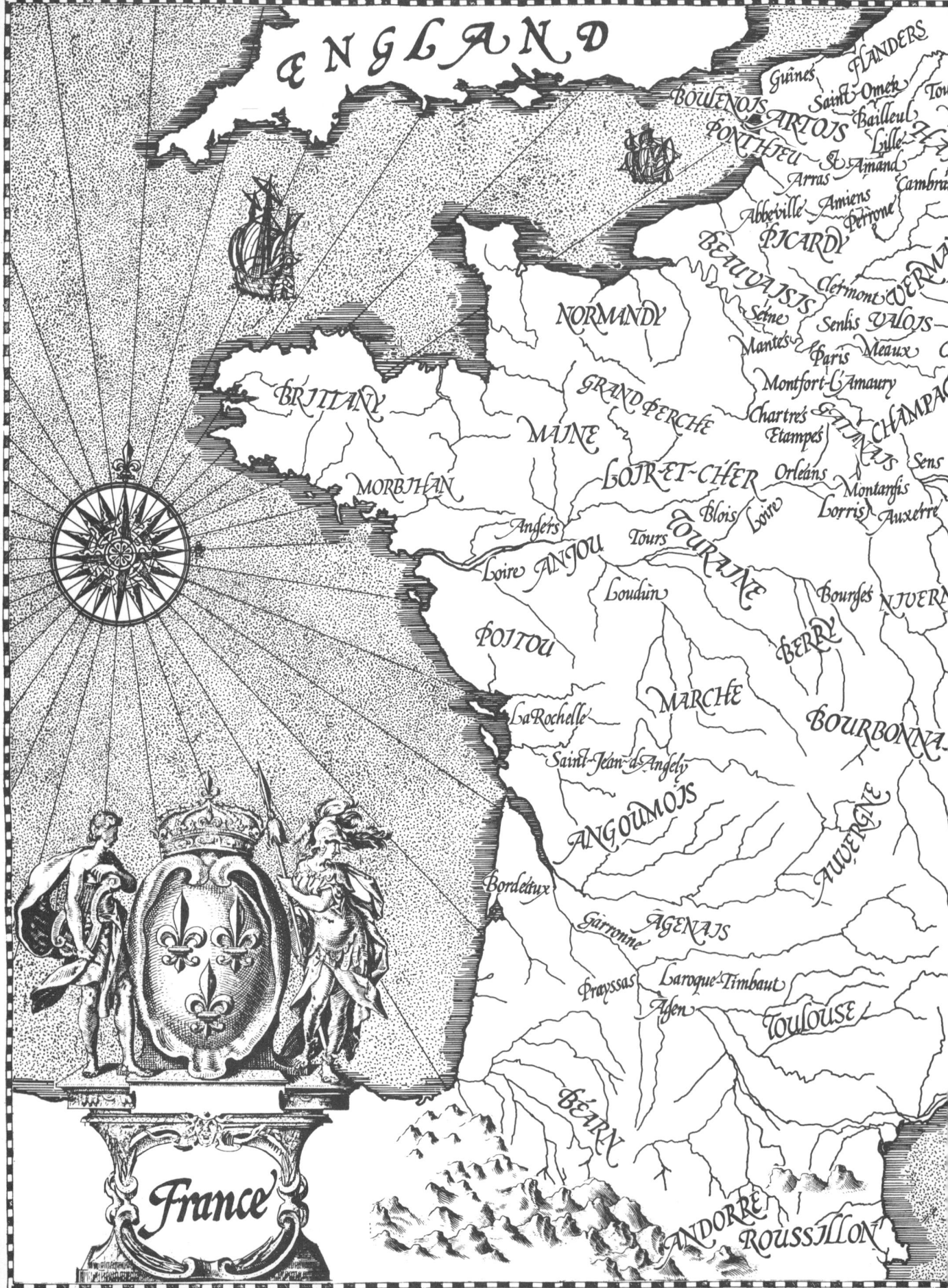

ENGLAND

FLANDERS
Guînes
Saint-Omer
BOULENOIS ARTOIS Bailleul
PONTHIEU St Amand Lille HA
Arras Cambrai
Abbeville Amiens
PICARDY Péronne
BEAUVAISIS Clermont WERMA
Sèine Senlis VALOIS
NORMANDY Mantes Paris Meaux
Montfort-L'Amaury
GRAND PERCHE Chartres GATINAIS CHAMPA
MAINE Etampes
BRITTANY LOIR-ET-CHER Orléans Sens
Blois Loire Montanfis
MORBIHAN Lorris Auxerre
Angers TOURAINE
Loire ANJOU Tours Bourges NIVER
Loudun BERRY
POITOU
MARCHE BOURBONNA
La Rochelle
Saint-Jean-d'Angely
ANGOUMOIS AUVERGNE
Bordeaux
Garronne AGENAIS
Prayssas Laroque-Timbaut
Agen TOULOUSE

France

Béarn
ANDORRE ROUSSILLON